ORCA WILD

GONE IS GONE

WILDLIFE UNDER THREAT

Foreword by **Jane Goodall**

Text and photographs by

ISABELLE GROC

ORCA BOOK PUBLISHERS

Library and Archives Canada Cataloguing in Publication

Title: Gone is gone: wildlife under threat / text and photographs by Isabelle Groc.
Names: Groc, Isabelle, author, photographer.

Description: Series statement: Orca wild | Includes bibliographical references and index.

Identifiers: Canadiana (print) 20190069317 | Canadiana (ebook) 20190069325 | ISBN 9781459816855
(hardcover) | ISBN 9781459816862 (PDF) | ISBN 9781459816879 (EPUB)

Subjects: LCSH: Endangered species—Juvenile literature. | LCSH: Rare animals—Juvenile literature.

Classification: LCC QL83 .G76 2019 | DDC j591.68—dc23

Library of Congress Control Number: 2019934034
Simultaneously published in Canada and the United States in 2019

Summary: This nonfiction book for middle readers looks at why and what species have become endangered,
how scientists are learning about endangered wildlife, what people are doing to conserve species and
what young people can do to help. Illustrated with unique photos by the photo-journalist author.

Orca Book Publishers is committed to reducing the consumption of nonrenewable resources in the making of our books.
We make every effort to use materials that support a sustainable future.

Orca Book Publishers gratefully acknowledges the support for its publishing programs provided by
the following agencies: the Government of Canada, the Canada Council for the Arts and the Province
of British Columbia through the BC Arts Council and the Book Publishing Tax Credit.

Cover and interior photographs: Isabelle Groc

Edited by Sarah N. Harvey
Design by Jenn Playford
Author photo by Elodie Doumenc

ORCA BOOK PUBLISHERS
orcabook.com

Printed and bound in China.

22 21 20 19 • 4 3 2 1

A snowy owl, one of the most iconic
Arctic-nesting birds, makes a rare
appearance in BC.

*This book is dedicated to my wonderful parents and life pillars,
René and Marie-Thérèse, who have always believed in me
and give me the strength of unconditional love;
to Lesley and her never-failing encouragement;
and to Elodie and Emile, who always inspire me to
share my love of wildlife.*

CONTENTS

FOREWORD

Isabelle Groc has done a great service for young people and our natural world by writing this book. She describes the threat to our planet's wildlife in a way that stresses the urgency of the situation we face today, providing scientific information but also describing, in a way that reaches the heart, the beauty that is vanishing.

Gone Is Gone was written primarily for a young audience, but it does not shy away from hard facts. The International Union for the Conservation of Nature (IUCN) publishes the Red List of threatened species every year, and the 2018 report provided chilling news: almost 97,000 animal and plant species are threatened, and almost 27,000 of these species are at risk of extinction.

It is human actions that have brought about this shocking situation, bringing us into what is known as the Sixth Great Extinction. Habitat destruction, pollution of air, land and water, reckless burning of fossil fuels and the disastrous effects of intensive agriculture have led to shrinking supplies of fresh water—and to climate change. And, in addition to all of this, there is the illegal trafficking of wildlife. We have lost approximately one half of the world's original forests and polluted the oceans—the two great "lungs" of the world, both now losing the ability to absorb carbon dioxide from the atmosphere and give out oxygen. Of all the mammals living on earth today, only about 4 percent are wild creatures. The rest are livestock and people—we are animals too.

But the main value of Isabelle's book lies in her infectious passion for the natural world and her belief that it is not too late to heal some of the scars we have inflicted. She is awestruck by the wonder of nature, and she shares the magic of the animal kingdom with young readers. Whether Isabelle is observing dolphins off the coast of Thailand or accompanying her children to release rare frogs into a wetland, her own efforts to protect what we have left is inspiring. The more we know about the life forms with which we share the planet, the more likely we are to want to save them. Isabelle doesn't simply say this. She lives it.

I always stress that *every single individual makes an impact on the planet—every single day.* And we humans can choose what sort of impact we make. Isabelle's most important and lasting message is also the most resonant: if human behavior is the cause of the wildlife crisis, it can also be the solution. Remember that you are not alone and that together we can save precious species. To which I would add: we *can* and we *MUST.* Before it is too late.

Jane Goodall, PhD, DBE
Founder, Jane Goodall Institute
and United Nations Messenger of Peace

A female grizzly bear shares her salmon catch in the fall with her two cubs on the west coast of BC.

INTRODUCTION

The blue whale is going extinct. I was playing in my parents' kitchen when I saw the news on the television. I was just a little girl, and it was the first time I had ever heard the word *extinct*. I did not know what it meant, but I knew there was something wrong. I grew up in a small town in the South of France where there was no ocean and no blue whales, but I still felt sad and angry. Blue whales are the largest of all animals that live on earth—over ninety-eight feet (thirty meters) long, even larger than most dinosaurs. Their tongues alone can weigh as much as an elephant. How could such a powerful creature disappear?

I found out that blue whales had been hunted to the point where there were almost none left. I wanted to do something to help the whales, and I found out that others also wanted to help. I saw news reports of people marching in the street, protesting against

The author holds an Oregon spotted frog, Canada's most endangered amphibian, in the Fraser Valley of BC. ALEESHA SWITZER

the hunting of the whales. Others joined an organization called Greenpeace, traveled in small inflatable boats on the high seas and placed themselves between the whalers' harpoons and the whales. Eventually governments listened, and in the 1980s there was a world-wide ban on commercial whaling. But even now whales are hunted by countries like Japan and Norway, which voted against the ban.

Many years later when I was in Mexico I saw a blue whale for the first time. Blue whales had not gone extinct, and I knew it was because some people had fought to save those whales during my childhood and had not given up. I felt grateful that the whales were still around, and it gave me hope that when we care for the wild, other *endangered species* can recover. This book tells the stories of a few of the species—from North Atlantic right whales to Oregon spotted frogs to African elephants—that are endangered and need our help. When you learn about them, you can start helping and make a difference, in the same way as others cared for our great whales before you were even born.

A Laysan albatross takes off from Midway Atoll National Wildlife Refuge. More than 70 percent of the world's population of the Laysan albatross nests on Midway.

WILD ENCOUNTER
Watching the run together

My daughter, Elodie, was only eight months old when I first took her to the Adams River in British Columbia to watch the millions of bright-red sockeye salmon return to the river to spawn and die. Since then a trip to the Adams River has become a family tradition every few years. We returned when Elodie was four years old and again when she was seven. That year she was joined by her baby brother, Emile. It was a peak year for the salmon run, and the fish were packed so tight in the river they could barely move. Their green heads were pushing forward while their tails were slapping on the water.

I feel so lucky that we get to experience this natural miracle as a family. Every time we go, I tell the children that Pacific salmon feed the entire **ecosystem**: bears, wolves, bald eagles, gulls, ravens, jays, insects—all come to feast on the salmon. I remind them that if there were no more salmon, many species would be in trouble. Elodie and Emile have begun to realize that all living things on earth fit together like a giant puzzle and depend on each other. In nature everything is connected, and when a species disappears, the balance maintained by all these connections is lost. We as humans lose too, because we are part of nature and depend on it. I hope these shared memories will inspire my children and others to stand up and protect our wildlife. As a matter of fact, Emile was just one year old when he attended his first environmental rally in Vancouver, British Columbia, to protect wild salmon.

A leopard in Etosha National Park, Namibia, is ready to pounce on its prey, a black-faced impala.

1

WILDLIFE UNDER THREAT

L ife in the wild is not always easy for animals. They can be attacked by other animals (including humans) that hunt them, and they must work hard to find enough food to survive. But now humans have made life tougher for many species. We clear the natural spaces where animals live to build cities, roads and farms. We hunt animals and pollute their *habitat*. Our climate has changed because of our increasing use of *fossil fuels* such as oil and coal, which release *carbon dioxide* and other *greenhouse gases* into the air. Species cannot keep up with these changes, and as a result many of them—in rainforests, oceans, mountains, deserts and the frozen lands of the North—have become endangered. Others are now extinct. Once a species becomes extinct it is gone forever, and the current rate of extinction is cause for alarm. Species are now going extinct faster than they used to, with consequences that we do not fully comprehend.

THE SIXTH MASS EXTINCTION

Mass extinctions are not new. We know that at least five have occurred in our planet's history over the last 500 million years. The most recent mass extinction wiped out the dinosaurs 65 million years ago, after a meteor strike. What these past extinctions had in common was that they were the result of catastrophic natural events. But now species are going extinct far faster than they used to. It is estimated that over the last century, extinction rates for species are at least 100 times higher than the "background" or "natural" extinction rate without human impact. Scientists warn that we are now in the middle of a sixth mass extinction, this one caused by humans. The Living Planet Index, which measures global diversity, indicates that worldwide populations of mammals, birds, fish, *amphibians* and *reptiles* declined by 60 percent between 1970 and 2014.

The marine iguana is the only lizard in the world with the ability to feed at sea and is found only on the Galapagos Islands.

GONE IS GONE

The passenger pigeon was a bird that lived in large migratory flocks in North America. People who saw them said the skies were sometimes black with pigeons because there were so many of them. But people killed them for food, and their natural habitat was taken over by farming. Each year the flocks of birds kept getting smaller, until the very last passenger pigeon, Martha, died at the Cincinnati Zoo in September 1914.

In 2006 scientists went on an expedition to search for the baiji, a dolphin that lived in the Yangtze River in China. It was very difficult for the dolphins to live close to people, especially once the river they lived in became polluted by industry. They were hit by boats and tangled in fishing nets. The scientists could not find any remaining dolphins, and the species was declared extinct. Extinction happens fast if we are not careful. The first step in preventing extinction is to learn about all these different species, to understand how important they are in the natural world and why they have become so vulnerable. Sadly, too many species simply disappear because nobody pays attention to them, and it then becomes too late to save them from extinction.

In the early 1800s the passenger pigeon had an estimated population of at least 3 billion birds. By 1900 the birds had been hunted to extinction.

THE RED LIST: MEASURING RISK

How do we know which species are in the most danger? A scientific organization called the International Union for Conservation of Nature (IUCN) publishes the Red List of Threatened Species ever year. The Red List is a "barometer of life." It helps governments, environmental organizations and scientific institutions plan for conservation actions by indicating which animals, plants and *fungi* are at risk of extinction and need protection.

The Red List uses a rigorous scientific process to assess species' extinction risk based on past, present and future threats. Every species on the Red List is given a category.

In 2018 more than 96,900 species were on the IUCN Red List, and more than 26,800 were threatened with extinction. But there are many more to check, and the IUCN's goal is to have 160,000 species assessed by 2020. Scientists have described over 1.6 million species on earth, and this figure increases all the time as more information is compiled. It would not be a surprise if many of these unchecked species are also found to be endangered.

A species is a group of similar individual animals that are able to reproduce. A single species may be known by different names in different languages. To avoid confusion, every species has a two-part scientific name in Latin. The system was created in the 1750s by Swedish scientist Carl Linnaeus, who named, ranked and classified plants and animals. He named over 12,000 species, and his system is still in use today.

Elephants congregate, bathe and play at a waterhole in Etosha National Park, Namibia.

THE RED LIST: MEASURING RISK

EXTINCT
Gone forever.

EXTINCT IN THE WILD
Survives only in captivity.

CRITICALLY ENDANGERED
Clings on in the wild in tiny numbers and is facing an extremely high risk of extinction.

ENDANGERED
In trouble and the risk of extinction is very high.

VULNERABLE
Already under threat and will become endangered if not protected.

NEAR THREATENED
Not in danger but could be soon.

SPECIES OF LEAST CONCERN
Appears to be safe for now.

DATA DEFICIENT
Not enough is known about species to determine whether it is endangered or not.

The snowy owl was classified as "vulnerable" for the first time on the IUCN Red List in 2017. Climate change is likely to be a significant threat, as it can affect the availability and distribution of the owl's prey.

Galapagos sea lions are vulnerable to climate change and disease and are assessed as "endangered."

LIFE ON THE EDGE

Have you ever heard of the long-beaked echidna? This mammal lays eggs like a bird, has a long tongue for poking into the ground to find ants and grows spines for protection. And what about the olm? It is a sightless, lungless, cave-dwelling salamander that can live without food for ten years. If these extraordinary animals become extinct, there will be nothing like them left on the planet. These species have few close relatives on the tree of life and are often unusual in the way they look, live and behave. They represent a unique and irreplaceable part of the world's natural heritage. Sadly, these weird animals are often poorly known and neglected. People don't pay much attention to them and do not protect them, perhaps because they are not cuddly or cute. As a result, many are now at risk of extinction. The Edge of Existence program, developed by the Zoological Society of London, is trying to change that. It has made a list of mammals, amphibians, corals, birds and reptiles that are both on the verge of extinction and "highly evolutionary distinct." The program supports field research expeditions to learn more about these species and conservation actions to secure their future.

WHY AND HOW DO SPECIES BECOME ENDANGERED?

Habitat Loss

The main reason why so many species become endangered is the widespread destruction of their habitat by humans. Can you imagine what it would be like to come home from school one day to find that your house was gone? What would you do? When the habitat of a plant

Because they fly low, at three to six feet (one to two meters) above ground, barn owls are often hit by cars when they cross roads to move from one grass patch to another or hunt along highways.

WILD ENCOUNTER
Vultures in trouble

When I first went to Africa vultures were a common sight. As nature's garbage collectors they clean up carcasses and contribute to a healthy environment. In Botswana I remember watching many white-backed vultures sitting on a single tree. I have always found vultures beautiful and fascinating, but they are often unloved and misunderstood. Yet they are very important. At the time I did not worry about them. But when I returned to Africa many years later, it was hard work to spot a single vulture. I know now that populations of vultures have suffered some of the fastest declines ever recorded in a bird. The white-backed vulture was the most common and widespread vulture in Africa, but in the span of fifty years the vulture population has declined by 90 percent; the white-backed vulture is now considered critically endangered. The main reason for the decline of many of the vulture species is poisoning. Farmers poison livestock carcasses to get rid of predators such as lions, leopards and hyenas, but the vultures eat the carcasses and die. Poachers also poison elephant and rhino carcasses to kill vultures, because they do not want hundreds of circling vultures alerting park rangers to a recently poached animal.

Forests around the world are under threat from deforestation, placing many animals that live in the forest at risk.

or animal is damaged or destroyed, there is nowhere for them to go. Species are losing their homes because of the growing needs of humans. Habitats are destroyed to make way for agriculture, housing, roads and activities such as mining and logging. Around half of the world's original forests have disappeared. Over 70 percent of the world's *wetlands* have been lost since 1900. A study published in May 2018 shows that of all mammals on earth, 60 percent are livestock and 36 percent are humans. Only 4 percent are wild mammals. Chickens and other farmed poultry now make up 70 percent of all birds on the planet, with just 30 percent being wild.

More people means fewer places for wildlife. As the human population grows and the natural habitats where wild animals live become smaller, people and animals are coming into conflict over living space and food. As villages and farms spread in Africa and Asia, tigers and lions have less natural *prey* to hunt, so they come closer to people and may eat farm livestock. The wild animals, many of which are already endangered, are often killed by people to prevent conflicts.

Pollution

Heavy metals, *pesticides* and other chemicals are all over the planet. They get into the air, soil and water and contaminate the wildlife. These chemicals can cause all sorts of problems. For example, a population of beluga whales lives in the St. Lawrence River in Quebec, near the highly industrialized Great Lakes region. Industrial pollutants have made the whales sick. They have become one of the most contaminated marine mammals in the world, with the highest rate of cancer ever reported in whales.

WILD ENCOUNTER
A curious northern spotted owl

A few years ago I traveled to Oregon to write a story on the northern spotted owl. These birds live in the **old-growth forests** of the Pacific Northwest, where they nest in holes in big old trees. Unfortunately, because of logging the old-growth forest has been disappearing, leaving the owls with no place to live. As I was walking through the forest with a biologist, I kept wondering if I would catch a glimpse of the rare bird. Finally we stopped by a group of old-growth trees. All was quiet in the forest. Within minutes a spotted owl flew in, landed on a tree only a few feet away and stared intensely at us with eyes the color of dark chocolate. Even though spotted owls have lost most of their world to logging, they are unafraid of humans. I looked at this gentle bird and felt we had betrayed its trust. It is our responsibility to do everything we can to save its habitat.

To kill the bugs they consider "pests," farmers and some gardeners spray pesticides on the plants they grow. But pesticides are poisons, and they have been making honey bees and other *pollinators* sick. The reduction in the population of pollinating insects is bad news for humans. Farmers depend on bees and other pollinators for the health and abundance of many of their crops, the source of our food.

Scientists are increasingly concerned with plastic *pollution* and particularly the impacts of *microplastics*—tiny pieces of plastic—found in the ocean. Growing numbers of marine animals, from fish to seabirds and whales, have microplastic in their bodies. Research shows that these tiny pieces of plastic can be transferred in the *food web* from one animal to another and possibly all the way to humans.

Climate Change

Earth is becoming warmer. *Climate change* and what it brings—melting glaciers, shrinking sea ice, rising sea levels, extreme weather—is affecting wildlife in many ways. In a rapidly warming world, the survival of many species depends on their ability to adapt, for example by migrating to new areas. But some species may not be able to adapt fast enough.

The Arctic is now warming at more than twice the rate of the rest of the planet, impacting the wildlife that lives there. The sea ice is home to several species, including polar bears, walruses, ringed seals and arctic foxes, and with little sea ice left the animals have nowhere to go. Polar bears hunt seals, rest and raise their young on the sea ice. Without ice and without seals to eat, the bears have a harder time surviving. They may have to search for other food. Sometimes they go to garbage dumps in villages, which creates conflicts between the bears and people. Female walruses

A rapidly warming Arctic is affecting Inuit communities that rely on ice to travel and hunt.

WILD ENCOUNTER
The albatross and the plastic bottle

Midway Atoll National Wildlife Refuge is located in the middle of the North Pacific Ocean, far away from humans. I traveled to this remote place to see both the beautiful Laysan and the black-footed albatrosses. Even though few people live on Midway, I was shocked to witness albatrosses nesting next to water bottles, cigarette lighters and fishing nets. Huge amounts of plastic end up in the ocean and float there for years, slowly releasing poisons into the water. The plastics are swept by ocean currents into massive garbage patches. Seabirds, turtles and even whales mistake the plastic for food, and it ends up obstructing their stomachs.

Sperm whales are particularly susceptible to ingesting plastic debris: they mistake debris for squid, their main prey. In 2018 a young sperm whale that had washed ashore on the southeast coast of Spain died after being unable to digest more than sixty pounds (twenty-seven kilograms) of plastic trash, fish netting and garbage bags in its stomach and intestines. The year of my visit, the Midway albatrosses fed their chicks about 4 tons (3.63 tonnes) of plastic. Every time I think of the albatrosses of Midway, I am reminded that it is our responsibility to recycle and reduce our use of plastic.

and their young spend the summer on floating sea ice, resting between dives to feed on clams, snails and marine worms in the offshore shallow waters of the Chukchi Sea. But now summer sea ice is melting more rapidly than ever before, and walruses abandon the ice and come ashore earlier and in bigger numbers. As walruses pack tightly onto beaches, any disturbance—the sound of an aircraft or the scent of a bear—can cause a deadly stampede. Young animals in particular are vulnerable to trampling injuries and death. Also, when on land walruses are far away from their best food sources and have to make long commutes to their feeding grounds.

The loss of sea ice during the summer makes some marine mammals more vulnerable to new *predators*. In the past orcas could not swim in ice-covered waters because of their large dorsal fins. Now they can access some areas in the Arctic, and they eat other marine mammals such as narwhals. The sea-ice loss also opens up opportunities

Each summer hundreds of narwhals return to the fjords and inlets of Baffin Bay in the Canadian Arctic.

for industrial development and commercial shipping in the region. Those activities bring more dangers to the local wildlife: oil pollution, ship strikes, noise.

Wildlife for Sale

Some species are endangered because they are hunted for sport or to sell for food or specific body parts. Fishing supports millions of people around the world. But in the last fifty years the oceans have been overfished, and fish populations have declined to a point where the survival of many species is uncertain. One example is the endangered Atlantic bluefin tuna, which is highly valued for sushi and sashimi.

Poaching is the illegal catching or killing of an animal on someone else's land or in contravention of official protection. Poachers may kill animals for their body parts, such as elephants for their ivory tusks, rhinoceroses for their horns and tigers for their bones and teeth. In some countries animal body parts are carved into decorative

Marine pollution is a serious threat to the endangered Hawaiian monk seal. Adults and pups can become entangled in marine debris and die as a result.

Hong Kong is the center of the global shark-fin trade. An estimated 73 million sharks are killed each year for their fins.

objects or used in traditional medicines. For example, the pangolin—a shy, toothless, insect-eating animal—is the most trafficked mammal in the world: the four Asian species have been hunted nearly to extinction, while the four African species are being poached in record numbers. In China and other East Asian nations, pangolin meat is considered an expensive delicacy, and pangolin is also used as an ingredient in traditional medicine.

Hunting wild animals for food is also a growing threat to many species. A wild animal sold as food is called *bushmeat*. Africa's great *apes* are captured illegally for bushmeat and are now close to extinction.

Each year rare animals are also caught so they can be sold to private zoos or to collectors who keep them as pets. For example, cheetahs are caught in Africa and transported to the Middle East, where some people keep them as luxury pets. Many of the animals suffer and die on the long journeys.

Many people are afraid of sharks, but today many shark species are endangered. They die because they accidentally get entangled in fishing nets, and they are also hunted for their fins to make shark-fin soup, a traditional Chinese dish. When I was in Hong Kong, I was sad to see so many shark fins in jars for sale everywhere in the city. The disappearance of sharks can negatively affect the whole ecosystem.

The Invaders: The World's Most Unwanted Species

When they go into the habitat of wild animals, people can accidentally or intentionally introduce plants and animals that do not belong in these places. When that happens the introduced species is capable of moving aggressively to an area and has the potential to compete with the *native species*, disrupting the natural balance that existed before the invader's introduction. Most species have predators in their natural habitat that keep their population in check, but when new species are introduced, they typically come without their natural predators. They are often hardier and more aggressive and reproduce faster than the native species. Some introduced animals also carry diseases that make the local wildlife even more vulnerable to endangerment. According to the IUCN, *invasive species* are the second most significant threat to *biodiversity* after habitat loss.

The Burmese python, one of the largest snakes in the world, is native to Asia. When it was introduced in Everglades National Park in Florida—likely released by people who owned the snakes as pets—this invasive species became a serious threat to the native wildlife, driving the decline of many mammals, birds and other reptiles.

One of the most devastating examples of the impacts of an invasive species is the Nile perch, a fish introduced into Lake Victoria in Africa in the 1950s. This led to the disappearance of more than 200 native fish species through predation and competition for food.

Red squirrels store nuts and seeds under logs, at the base of trees and underground. Because they do not eat all stored food, they help spread seeds in the forest.

Native to eastern North America, the gray squirrel may look cute, but when it invades other regions this small mammal has destructive impacts. First introduced in the 1870s in the United Kingdom, the gray squirrel has become one of the country's worst nightmares. The squirrels are destructive to native trees as they can strip them of their protective bark, leaving them vulnerable to disease. They are also larger and more aggressive than the native red squirrels and outcompete them. Rivalry between the two squirrel species is not the only problem: the gray squirrel is a carrier of the squirrel pox, *parapoxvirus*, which is deadly to the red squirrel but seemingly harmless to the gray.

Both the Nile perch and the gray squirrel made it to the list "100 of the World's Worst Invasive Alien Species," published by the Invasive Species Specialist Group, which illustrates the variety of species that have the ability to travel and become established, thrive and dominate in new places. Once an invasive species is present, it takes a lot of effort and time to get rid of it.

The American bullfrog, native to Eastern Canada, was accidentally introduced to British Columbia fifty years ago. These large frogs eat the endangered Oregon spotted frog and other smaller frogs. *Wetlands* where bullfrogs are found have much smaller populations of native amphibians.

The American bullfrog, Canada's largest amphibian, is one of the world's most invasive species.

FACING THE THREAT OF EXTINCTION

African Elephants

Watching a herd of elephants at a watering hole in Africa is a unique experience. Elephants love water! They don't just drink it, but also bathe and play in it. I watched one elephant climb on the back of another and then splash into the water. There were tiny calves at the watering hole, and seeing the animals interact with one another reminded me that elephants live in families with strong relationships. Every day humans impact the lives of wild elephants. Tens of thousands of animals are killed every year for their ivory tusks. As the human population expands more land is converted to agriculture. So elephant habitat is destroyed, and the animals get too close to people. Sometimes they go into farmers' fields, damage the crops and are killed. They have also been exploited for entertainment in circuses around the world and forced to give tourists rides.

In Africa dedicated groups are doing everything they can to defend elephants against ivory poachers and traffickers. The Black Mamba Anti-Poaching Unit is an anti-poaching team, made up of mostly women, working to save elephants in South Africa. Since 2013 the Black Mambas have patroled the Balule Nature Reserve (part of the Greater Kruger National Park) by foot or Jeep to track suspicious poaching activities. In Africa and Asia, conservation groups work to reduce elephant-human conflicts. They have learned that elephants are scared of bees, so *conservationists* have used this fear to protect the elephants. Beehives are placed on farmland, and as result the elephants stay away, so do no damage to crops, and therefore farmers are less likely to shoot them.

Ten million elephants used to roam across Africa, but poaching and habitat destruction have dramatically reduced their population. Today there are less than half a million left in Africa.

Elephants are social animals with a strong sense of family. Families live together for their entire lives, under the leadership of an elder matriarch.

Koalas

The koala, one of the most famous inhabitants of Australia, is struggling. The bushland where koalas live is being destroyed by bushfires or to make way for houses. Following habitat destruction, koalas spend more time on the ground than in trees and so are more vulnerable to domestic dog attacks and vehicle strikes. In 2012 Australia placed the koala on the vulnerable-species list. Koalas have also been hard hit by an epidemic of chlamydia infections. Chlamydia causes painful urinary tract inflammation, infertility and blindness. The Koala Hospital, located in Port Macquarie in New South Wales, admits between 200 and 250 sick or injured koalas every year. The Australian Koala Foundation is a strong advocate for koalas and

Koalas live in eastern Australia, where they feed on the leaves of eucalyptus trees, their favorite food. They rarely leave the trees and sleep for up to 18 hours a day.

is lobbying for the enactment of a Koala Protection Act that will save koala forests.

Kangaroos

Most people are familiar with the red kangaroo, Australia's national symbol. It is less known that Australia actually has approximately fifty-eight species of kangaroos. Another twenty species are found in New Guinea. There are three family groups: kangaroos, wallabies, pademelons and tree-kangaroos are one family (Macropodidae); potoroos, bettongs and rat-kangaroos are another family (Potoroidae); and one single species, the musky rat-kangaroo, is the only surviving member of its own family (Hypsiprymnodontidae).

The smallest kangaroo species have suffered the fastest declines in the last 200 years. Seven species are now extinct, and many others are declining significantly. Species are threatened by habitat loss and degradation, as well as by introduced predators such as the European red fox and *feral* cats. Both cats and foxes will take on wallabies weighing up to about thirteen pounds (six kilograms). The critically endangered Gilbert's potoroo is the world's rarest marsupial and Australia's rarest mammal, found only in Western Australia. It lost much of its habitat to fire and clearing for agriculture, and was also preyed on by introduced red foxes and feral cats. The endangered Proserpine rock-wallaby is confined to a very small area in central coastal Queensland. The animals are threatened by increasing tourism and residential development, and are also attacked by pet dogs and run over on roads.

Madagascar's Lemurs

Black-and-white ruffed lemurs are one of over 100 species of lemurs that are only found in Madagascar. On this

Koalas eat a lot for their size—about 2.5 pounds (just over 1 kilogram) of eucalyptus leaves a day. They do not drink much water, so they get most of the moisture they need from the tree leaves.

The black-and-white ruffed lemur is among the largest living lemurs in Madagascar and is also one of the largest pollinators in the world. As the lemurs feed, pollen sticks to the ruffs of fur around their faces and gets carried from tree to tree.

island located off the east coast of Africa, lemurs evolved separately from other primates. Lemurs are not the only critters that are unique in Madagascar. Over 90 percent of Madagascar's reptiles, plant life and mammals exist nowhere else on earth. Yet lemurs are one of the world's most endangered animals. The black-and-white ruffed lemur is listed as "critically endangered," as are many other species of lemurs. The biggest threat to lemurs is the destruction of the forest where they live. They are also overhunted.

Local and international conservation groups are trying to help local people protect lemurs in Madagascar, one of the poorest countries in the world. They help communities living around protected areas find new ways to make a living without destroying forests or hunting lemurs. Some projects are working to reforest the island, creating jobs for the local residents, who are helping rebuild lemur habitat.

Lions

As a child I thought lions were invincible—nothing could defeat them. When I saw a pair of lions for the first time, peacefully resting under the shade of a tree in the African heat, my heart was racing. It turns out that lions, like many other species, have become more fragile because of humans. They used to live in most of Africa, Southern Europe and the Middle East all the way to northwestern India. Now their habitat has been reduced to a few tiny pockets in sub-Saharan Africa and in the Gir forest of India. Many initiatives aim to protect the remaining lion populations. In Kenya, Ewaso Lions is dedicated to conserving lions by helping local people live with lions. Project Leonardo, a program led by Panthera, an American organization committed to saving the world's big cats,

The African lion population decreased by 43 percent between 1993 and 2014, due to loss of habitat, bushmeat hunting and conflict with humans.

WILD ENCOUNTER
The world's tallest animal

It is always a special experience to see giraffes in Africa. They seem to dominate the landscape with their gentle gracefulness. Watching giraffes drink at a watering hole in Namibia's Etosha National Park reminded me of their fragility. They approach the watering hole very slowly, look around for any sign of nearby danger (such as lions or leopards), spread their front legs and lower their heads to the water's surface. While they are drinking, they look like ballet dancers showcasing a particularly acrobatic movement. Getting their heads near the water makes them vulnerable, since getting up quickly in the event of danger is not easy.

Between 1985 and 2015, giraffe numbers have declined, mostly because of habitat loss, illegal hunting and civil wars in many parts of Africa. In 2016 the IUCN changed the giraffe's status from "least concern" to "vulnerable" on its Red List. Scientists call this decline a "silent extinction" because until recently they did not pay much attention to giraffes, did not realize they were in trouble and did not know much about them. Now scientists are doing more research to better protect Africa's tallest animals. In Kenya scientists with the Giraffe Conservation Foundation and other organizations have attached tiny, solar-powered GPS trackers on top of the heads of some reticulated giraffes—a distinct species—to learn more about their habitat and what they need to survive.

works to reduce human-lion conflict and fights illegal hunting in several African countries where lions still exist.

Cheetahs

Cheetahs, the fastest land animals on earth, are struggling in the race against extinction. Once found throughout Africa and in much of Asia and numbering around 100,000 animals in 1900, cheetahs are now persisting in a very small percentage of their historic *range*. The global population is now estimated at about 7,000 animals. Namibia has the world's largest subpopulation of cheetahs, almost 4,000. Because of conflicts with more powerful predators such as lions and hyenas, which kill cheetahs' cubs and steal their food, most cheetahs live outside protected reserves and parks, including on farmland. There they encounter other dangers. Cheetahs live close to humans who are raising

One of the most distinctive features of a cheetah's face is the black tear stripe that runs from each eye to the mouth. The stripes are thought to protect the cheetah's eyes from the sun's glare.

cows, sheep and goats, and they are often held responsible for the loss of farm animals, even when those animals may have been killed by other predators such as leopards or hyenas. As a result Namibian farmers have felt they have no option but to kill the big cats to protect their livestock. Between 1980 and 1990, nearly 10,000 cheetahs were lost that way, according to the Cheetah Conservation Fund, an organization that works to reduce conflicts between farmers and cheetahs in Namibia.

The cheetah is the fastest land animal on earth. With its long legs and slender body, it can achieve an unbelievable top speed of 68 miles (110 kilometers) per hour.

The northern spotted owl lives in the old-growth forests of the Pacific Northwest.

UNDERSTANDING ENDANGERED SPECIES

2

It is not always clear why a species is in trouble. To better protect endangered species, scientists first need to understand them. They have to conduct research not only to learn how many animals are left, but also to discover where they live, how they move around, how long they live, what they eat and how often they reproduce. Sometimes animals are shy and do not want to be seen or studied, so scientists have to find ways to track these species without disturbing them. While some species, such as elephants, are well studied, many are difficult to access. Try to imagine studying whales in the ocean. Since they spend most of their lives below the sea's surface, well out of human sight, it takes dedication and skill to study them.

RESEARCH IN THE FIELD

When it comes to studying a species, scientists can be like detectives. They travel the world and look for species during long field expeditions that take them to the depths of lakes and oceans, through tropical jungles, across deserts, up mountains or down rivers. Sometimes species that were long lost and thought to be extinct are rediscovered during these expeditions. The Cuban greater funnel-eared bat was thought to be extinct until a population was rediscovered in a single remote cave in Cuba. In 2017 the Jackson's climbing salamander was found in the mountains of Guatemala. This small salamander, also known as the golden wonder, had not been seen in forty-two years. The discovery was part of a campaign to search the world for species that have

Elodie is learning to band a barn owl chick in the Fraser Valley of BC.

Biologist Lauren Meads is banding a juvenile burrowing owl as part of a program to reintroduce the species to BC's grasslands.

been lost to science. The golden wonder was among the twenty-five most-wanted species on that list.

When looking for species, field researchers interview local people and conduct what are called *line transects*, where they follow a line for a set distance and count the animals they see. They undertake surveys by boat and plane. During the Great Elephant Census in 2014 and 2015, dozens of researchers flew in small planes to count elephants in eighteen countries.

Smile! You Are on Camera!

The first step in understanding an animal is to watch it in the wild, but it is not always possible to do that. *Nocturnal* (active only at night) animals are especially difficult to observe. Scientists set up hidden cameras called *camera traps* to capture images of these creatures. The traps have motion sensors that activate the camera when an animal walks past. The gray-faced sengi, a giant elephant-shrew mammal living in the mountains of Tanzania, was first discovered with camera traps.

Volunteers are doing a night survey on Vancouver Island, counting amphibians on the road.

ASK THE LOCALS!

Scientists can rarely spend enough time with a specific animal to witness all its behaviors. Because they only conduct studies for a limited time during the summer, more scientists now work with Indigenous peoples to learn about wildlife. In the Arctic hunters are traveling, hunting, boating and observing wildlife on the land and ocean throughout the year. As a result Indigenous peoples have a lot of knowledge they can share. One summer an Inuit hunter paddling next to a resting narwhal in Greenland observed a thin layer coming off the narwhal's body and dissipating in the water. The event lasted only a few seconds, but a narwhal researcher based in the United States realized the scientific importance of the hunter's discovery: whereas the beluga, the narwhal's nearest relative, is known to enter warmer estuaries in the summer to molt, this skin-renewal process had never been scientifically documented for narwhal, in part because no scientist had spent sufficient time in remote Arctic locations to record such an event. The local hunter's observation made a difference!

Yupik whalers on St. Lawrence Island in Alaska helped improve census methods for bowhead whales by telling scientists they could not see all the whales from the edge of the ice. They also shared insights on bowheads' ability to swim through the ice where they cannot be seen. In the eastern Canadian Arctic, scientists knew very little about the hunting tactics of orcas (killer whales) until they asked Inuit hunters. They learned that orcas use specific methods to hunt bowheads, belugas, narwhals and seals, and they discovered at least two different killer whale groups based on what they preferred to eat.

In Nunavut scientists rely on the insights provided by the Inuit people who live close to Arctic wildlife.

WILD ENCOUNTER
Waiting for the sea unicorn

Narwhals are one of the most mysterious animals on the planet. Because of their single tusk, many people just know the narwhals as sea unicorns. The Arctic, where the narwhals live, is changing, and scientists are worried about the narwhals' future. To protect them, scientists need to learn more about their behavior, where they go and what they eat. But narwhals are particularly difficult to study because they spend the winter under the ice, in complete darkness. Nobody can go there and observe them, so scientists use satellite transmitters to learn more about their lives.

One summer I joined a two-week expedition in Tremblay Sound, a remote place in Baffin Bay in the Canadian Arctic. Every year hundreds of narwhals travel to the fjords and inlets of Baffin Bay, and scientists hoped to catch animals as they swam past our camp and then attach satellite transmitter tags to them.

When we arrived at Tremblay Sound, there was nothing there but rocks, a little vegetation and a constant wind. I wondered if we could even survive there, but a day later the site was transformed into a research station, with colorful tents for sleeping in, a kitchen tent and a science lab. I remember when I saw my very first group of narwhals swimming past our camp. There were hundreds of them, some of them females with calves, traveling fast, and I could see tusk tips coming out of the water. I even saw a full tusk that stayed out of the water for a few minutes, then slowly moved down like the mast of a sinking boat.

During our expedition we managed to catch and tag five narwhals. One of them was a large female. The researchers worked fast to attach a tag to her back. They also collected a small piece of skin, monitored her heart rate, took a blood sample and measured her body size. In less than thirty minutes the animal was ready to be released. Tags mounted on narwhals transmit signals picked up by satellites high above the earth. For several months the tags give researchers information on where the narwhals go, how deep they dive and how long they stay underwater. Every single piece of information helps protect the narwhal in a fast-changing Arctic environment.

A team of scientists catches and attaches a satellite transmitter to a narwhal in the Canadian Arctic. It will let them learn more about where narwhals go, how deep they dive and how long they can stay underwater.

A high-school student surveys amphibian egg masses in a wetland in the Fraser Valley of BC.

Around the world dedicated local people volunteer their time to observe and collect data on wildlife in their neighborhoods and share what they learn with scientists. In the small community of Ryder Lake in Chilliwack, British Columbia, Steve Clegg grew up with frogs, toads and salamanders. He was always fascinated with the creatures he could find in his parents' backyard and remembers catching tadpoles in the pond on the family property. He knew everything there was to know about local amphibians. As an adult, he became concerned about the high mortality of amphibians on roads, and he started volunteering for the Fraser Valley Conservancy's Ryder Lake Amphibian Protection Program.

Every summer fingernail-sized juvenile western toads begin their migration from the wetland where they were born to the forest where they live out the rest of their lives.

These juvenile western toads are on their migratory journey from the wetland to the forest.

Juvenile western toads are aggregating in a wetland before their migration to the forest.

WILD ENCOUNTER
Searching for the precious frog

With its bright golden eyes, the Oregon spotted frog is truly beautiful. No wonder its Latin name is *Rana pretiosa*, which means "precious frog." It is Canada's most endangered amphibian—and also one of the most difficult to find. The precious frog spends most of its time underwater and is very good at hiding under vegetation and in tunnels. They are so difficult to find that Oregon spotted frogs were once believed to be gone from Canada until a naturalist stumbled upon one during a survey of wetlands in British Columbia.

Oregon spotted frogs are now found only in British Columbia's Fraser Valley. Their numbers have declined by as much as 90 percent because of the loss of their wetland habitat to agriculture and urban development and also because of pollution and competition from invasive species such as the American bullfrog.

I always enjoy going out in my chest waders with the biologists for a day in the mud during frog breeding season in the spring. Every year biologists count all the egg masses the frogs lay. They also set hundreds of traps in the water that they check daily. Any frog caught in a trap is weighed, measured and equipped with a tag the size of a grain of rice before it is released and recaptured in the future. With this information researchers can learn about the survival of frogs and how the population is doing over time.

Scientists want to discover other places the frogs live that they don't know about. But trying to discover new populations of Oregon spotted frogs is time consuming for people because the frogs are so good at hiding. This is why scientists are now using **environmental DNA (eDNA)** sampling to search for new populations. As they interact with their environment, frogs and other species leave traces of biological material, which contains their unique DNA, in the water. These are great clues for the researchers, who can take small samples of water from different wetlands, analyze the samples in a lab and detect whether amphibians were there.

The annual summer migration is a dangerous journey for the tiny toads, as they often end up being squished by passing cars. Steve and other volunteers realized that in order to help the toads they needed to collect some data. They spent countless nights in cold and rainy conditions, identifying and counting amphibians on the roads of the neighborhood. Ten-year-old Sigourney de Jong along with other kids and her local nature club were some of the volunteers who joined a night amphibian road survey. Eventually the data Steve and other volunteers collected night after night helped the Fraser Valley Conservancy identify the main migration corridors western toads and other amphibians use when they cross the road. A toad tunnel was then built for the amphibians to cross the road safely.

Sigourney de Jong collects juvenile western toads in a bucket to help them cross the road.

Western toad populations have declined because of habitat destruction and road deaths.

Pips, an Australian cattle dog from the Conservation Canines program, looks for ermine scat in Haida Gwaii, BC.

Dogs: The Scientist's Best Friend

When studying an endangered animal, one of the best things to have is their poop (or scat)! Droppings contain information about what a creature eats, how healthy it is, any disease it may have and its stress levels. The only problem is that it can be difficult to find scat, especially for species that roam over large areas. It's like looking for a needle in a haystack, and this is why scientists are increasingly recruiting dogs and their keen sense of smell to help them.

In Washington State the Conservation Canines program has been training dogs to track down the scat of endangered animals all over the world. Sometimes dogs can be the last resort for locating species that are almost impossible to find otherwise. In Haida Gwaii in British Columbia, a local biologist spent years looking for a rare ermine. Nothing was known about the size of its population, its diet or its habitat. The biologist tried every method he could think of to find ermines. Nothing worked until a dog showed up. Pips, an Australian cattle dog, worked in Haida Gwaii's forest to find ermine scat, walking alongside creeks, jumping over logs and sniffing under woody debris. Pips visited twenty-five different sites over a period of two weeks, seeking scat the size of a broken-up match. By the end of the project he had managed to find eleven scat samples, and every time he found one, he was rewarded with a ball to fetch. Pips was so energetic, fast and focused, I had a hard time keeping up with him in the forest!

SMALL BOATS, BIG OCEANS

Researchers often use boats and planes to count and observe animals. It takes a lot of time, patience and commitment to search an area and find the animals. Think about how big the oceans are. Whales and dolphins spend a lot of time underwater and far from the shore, and it can be difficult to keep up with them when you are a human in a small boat.

I once spent time with researchers looking for the Irrawaddy dolphin in Thailand. In many parts of Asia, the dolphins are in trouble because they get entangled in fishing nets. Unfortunately, people don't know much about them. We traveled by boat in Thailand to find the dolphins. Every thirty minutes we stopped the boat to record information such as the temperature and the *salinity* (salt content) of the water so we could learn more about the dolphins' habitat. We also interviewed local fishermen about their knowledge of the dolphins. For five days we did not see any dolphins. All we saw were a few birds, leaping fish, jellyfish and floating trash. The weather was not cooperating either, and the wind sometimes forced us to go back

Sri Lankan marine mammal expert Anouk Ilangakoon takes water samples to learn more about the Irrawaddy dolphin habitat in Thailand.

Biologist Robin Baird and his team from Cascadia Research conduct a boat survey of marine mammals in Hawaii.

to port early. It was only on my last day that I finally saw a group of Irrawaddy dolphins for the first time. They were very far away, and all I saw was a flash of dark gray on the surface of the water for a short moment. I left Thailand, and the researchers continued their search.

Sometimes animals surprise the people who work so hard to study them. Every summer North Atlantic right whales visit the Bay of Fundy (between the Canadian provinces of New Brunswick and Nova Scotia) to socialize and feed on tiny creatures called *zooplankton* that are invisible to the human eye. Year after year researchers have learned to expect the whales in the Bay of Fundy. They have studied and photographed the animals since 1980. But things started to change. In 2013 only five whales came to the Bay of Fundy. Where had the whales gone? And why did they move? Researchers suspect that the food the whales eat has moved—possibly because of climate change and warming waters. When that happens, the whales follow and change their itinerary.

It became urgent to learn where the whales went, because if researchers don't know where the animals are, they cannot take actions to protect them. Researchers asked fishermen and other mariners to help them spot whales. They also conducted intensive boat and air surveys, and they found that the whales were moving north, with more animals showing up in the Gulf of St. Lawrence, a busy place where there are a lot of ships and fishing activity.

Underwater Spies: Listening for Whale Talk

I remember quietly sitting in an inflatable boat on the Churchill River in Manitoba. I could hear chirps, whistles and clicks coming from the water. We were surrounded

WILD ENCOUNTER
Thar she blows!

I love hearing the sound whales make when they blow. I am always excited because the sound is the signal that a whale is surfacing and I am going to see it! The blow has a distinctive smell, too, which always makes me wonder what the whales have been eating to have such bad breath! Blows are different in height and shape, and on a calm day on the water you can identify a species just by its blow. For example, North Atlantic right whales have a V-shaped blow. The breath of whales and dolphins contains a lot of useful information, and researchers are interested in obtaining small amounts of whales' blow vapor.

I watched researchers collect blow samples from North Atlantic right whales. It is not easy! One researcher pilots the boat carefully to approach the whales without disturbing them, and another stands at the bow, operating a long pole to catch droplets of blow vapor over the blowholes of the whales. Once the sample is collected, a third team member quickly labels the sample and stores it in a cooler. Back at the lab the researchers will analyze the samples and look for stress hormones. They want to measure stress because when animals become stressed as a result of human activities, their health and their ability to reproduce can be compromised.

In Puget Sound, Washington State, an endangered southern resident killer whale spy-hops to take a look around.

by beluga whales, and it felt like being in a jungle full of tropical birds. Nicknamed the canaries of the sea, belugas are one of the most vocal whale species.

Scientists have developed technologies to listen for whale calls so they can detect where the animals are. They have deployed underwater robots called gliders that are equipped with *hydrophones*. The robots automatically detect whale sounds, identify the species on the basis of the characteristics of the calls and report in real time, to scientists onshore, which species have been heard. These high-tech tools are a huge help for scientists trying to track the whereabouts of the endangered North Atlantic right whale. If they know where the whales are, scientists can more effectively reduce the dangers posed to these animals, such as being struck by ships or entangled in fishing gear, as a result of human activities.

A researcher checks the North Atlantic Right Whale Catalog to identify the whales he is seeing.

I Knew Your Mother: Whale Photo-Identification

Researchers can learn how an endangered species is doing over time by taking photographs of as many individuals as possible. Whales and dolphins have their own unique identifiers, such as the shape and size of their dorsal fins or the markings on their tails. Researchers photograph these unique identifiers and also record the date, time and location of their observations.

The photo-identification of orcas on the coast of British Columbia and Washington State started in the early 1970s. Year after year researchers have followed individual whales. They have learned about their behaviors, their social life and where they go. Researchers also notice changes due to human activities in the orcas' habitat. One of the most well known and beloved members of the southern resident killer whale population in the Pacific Northwest was J2, known as Granny. She had a distinguishing cut in her fin and was believed to be the world's oldest known orca. Her exact age was not known, although for a long time I believed she was born in 1911, the same year as my own grandmother. Every whale watcher in the region knew her. Granny was last seen in October 2016 and is now considered dead, heartbreaking news for all who enjoyed watching her for decades.

Since the early 1970s the New England Aquarium in Boston has maintained a catalog of North Atlantic right whales. Right whales can be individually identified by the unique patterns of callosities—roughened patches of skin—on their heads. Each whale is given a number and sometimes a name. The photographs that researchers take every year provide information about where the whales can be found in different seasons, when and where they

A researcher measures a northern Pacific rattlesnake in the Okanagan region of BC. The data collected in this study will help scientists understand how urban development and other forms of human disturbance affect the snakes.

have calves, how long they live, whether they have scars from entanglement with fishing gear, and more.

FROM FIELD RESEARCH TO ADVOCACY

In 1960 a young woman named Jane Goodall went to Tanzania to study the remarkable lives of chimpanzees. Equipped with a notebook and binoculars, she discovered that chimps made simple tools at a time when it was thought that only humans made and used tools. Her observations changed our knowledge and perceptions of chimpanzees. But now the survival of the species is threatened by habitat destruction and illegal trafficking. Jane continues her work to save the chimpanzees from extinction. She travels 300 days per year to speak to people around the world and inspire them to take action to conserve our natural world.

A biologist attaches a geolocator to a yellow-breasted chat, a migratory songbird whose range extends throughout southern Canada, the United States, Mexico and Central America. The data collected by the lightweight device allows scientists to learn more about the migratory journey of the bird.

WILD ENCOUNTER
Face-to-face with an entangled whale

A few years ago I stayed in a remote lodge in Gwaii Haanas National Park Reserve in British Columbia. One morning I was woken up by a loud splash that disturbed the calm, green waters around the lodge. I grabbed my camera and rushed outside to see what was happening. The noise was being made by a massive humpback whale repeatedly breaching right in front of us. I started taking photographs but after a few shots noticed that a rope was wrapped tightly around the whale's body. This animal was not performing acrobatics: it was frantically trying to free itself.

We immediately called the British Columbia Marine Mammal Response Network (BCMMRN), which responds to reports of sick, injured, dead and disturbed animals. Humpback whales used to be hunted, and they became almost extinct in the first half of the twentieth century. Now the whales are no longer hunted, but they face another danger: entanglement in fishing equipment such as ropes and nets. This was the first report the BCMMRN had ever received from Haida Gwaii regarding an entangled humpback whale, and a team was dispatched to try to find the animal. Unfortunately, the whale could not be located again in this area's intricate coastline, and its fate remains unknown.

Humpback whales are not the only whales to suffer. I have spent time on the east coast of Canada and the United States, photographing the endangered North Atlantic right whale. As I watched them I saw that many of the whales had scars. I remember a whale that we nicknamed Rudolph because it had a white spot on the front of its head—a scar from an entanglement in fishing equipment. According to scientists, the majority of right whales have been entangled during their lifetime.

To save the right whales from extinction, fishing practices have to change. Solving the problem of whale entanglement in fishing gear is difficult. Fishermen use rope, but when there is rope in the ocean, fishing grounds become minefields for the whales. Conservationists and researchers are working on various solutions to reduce entanglement. A study has shown that red and orange ropes are more visible to North Atlantic right whales, which could help them avoid entanglements. Scientists are also working on fishing ropes that can more easily break when whales become entangled in them. The Canadian government has changed the dates of the crab-fishing season so that fishing gear is out of the water by the time the whales are present. However, the best solution to this problem is to completely get rid of the ropes that are in the path of whales, which could be made possible by implementing ropeless fishing gear. In the meantime, efforts to disentangle whales have increased around the world. The volunteer-run Campobello Whale Rescue Team in New Brunswick (which consists primarily of fishermen) has disentangled many large whales since its creation in 2002.

A humpback whale struggles to free itself from a rope wrapped around its body.

The western painted turtle is BC's only remaining native freshwater turtle.

SAVING ENDANGERED SPECIES

3

I f human behavior is the cause of the wildlife crisis, it can also be the solution to the problem. When blue whales were on the edge of extinction, people started campaigns to stop whaling. These actions give us hope for many other endangered animals and remind us of what can be achieved when governments and local communities work together to protect species under threat. Thanks to the dedication of people who did not want to give up, some species that were once on the brink of extinction have been brought back.

People have been advocating for the protection of the natural world for a long time, and some of these early conservationists still inspire us today. In the nineteenth century John Muir was a naturalist and a strong advocate for the protection of natural areas. He wrote articles about the degradation of mountain meadows and forests. His writings influenced Congress to create a number of national parks in the United States. Rachel Carson was an American marine biologist who wrote an important book in the 1960s called *Silent Spring*, which talked about the dangers of chemical pesticides, especially DDT. Her work encouraged the United States to ban DDT and initiated the contemporary environmental movement.

Many others are working today to make things better for endangered wildlife and are taking many types of actions to conserve endangered species. You can help too!

WHY SAVE SPECIES?

The world's wild spaces and the creatures that live in them all benefit us. These benefits, which most of us do not even notice, are called *ecosystem services*. Our water, food and the air we breathe depend on the complex interactions of many different species in healthy habitats. For example, many of our crop plants would not survive and would not provide us with food without pollinators like bees and butterflies. So a lot of people are working hard to make sure pollinators survive. Unfortunately, insects are in trouble around the world.

In Germany a study has found that the number of flying insects has declined by 75 percent in twenty-five years. Their disappearance has significant consequences for the natural world, for humans and for the ecosystem services insects provide. Insects are not only pollinators but are also a source of food for many animals: birds, bats, fish and amphibians all eat bugs. Fewer bugs mean fewer other

The eastern bumblebee is a pollinator of flowers and numerous fruit and vegetable crops. Bees and other pollinators form the foundation of the food chain for other species, including humans.

animals. In France bird populations across the countryside have fallen by a third in just seventeen years because the insects on which they depend for food have disappeared. The decline in insects is due to several factors, including habitat destruction and urbanization, but the primary one is the intense use of pesticides on agricultural crops. Of particular concern is the use of a special class of pesticides called *neonicotinoids*, which have been linked to declining bee populations.

Another example of ecosystem services is the role forests play in regulating the climate by storing and isolating greenhouse gases. As trees and plants grow, they remove carbon dioxide from the atmosphere and lock it away in their tissues. Ecosystems such as wetlands filter waste through the biological activity of microorganisms in the soil and eliminate harmful *pathogens* (microbes that cause disease).

Ecosystems are also important for regulating pests and diseases that attack plants, animals and people. Predators and parasites—such as birds, bats, fungi and frogs—all act as natural controls and regulate pests and diseases. Birds of prey like the American kestrel, a small falcon species, eat numerous pests such as grasshoppers, rodents and European starlings that damage crops in agricultural areas. In Michigan researchers have installed nest boxes to attract falcons to cherry orchards and blueberry fields. They hope this will encourage farmers to stop using harmful pesticides to get rid of the pests that destroy their crops and let falcons do the job instead. Reducing pesticide use would help insects recover, as well as all the life on earth that they support.

We are part of nature, and protecting habitats and species comes down to saving ourselves. Studies show that the simple act of observing nature has a positive impact on

Barn owls can help control rodents. A nesting barn owl pair and their chicks eat 1,400 to 3,000 small rodents per year.

our health and well-being and makes us happier. People who live in areas with lots of birds, shrubs and trees are less likely to suffer from depression, anxiety and stress.

Species, even the smallest ones, can be precious indicators of how healthy our planet is and tell us when something is wrong with the environment, which can affect us all. For example, snails are disappearing at an alarming rate all over the world. If snails that live in the ocean have trouble building their shells (made of calcium carbonate), that means there are larger problems with the ocean, such as *ocean acidification*. On land, snails often live in habitats where they require specific features to survive: certain levels of moisture, shade and food. When snails do not have such conditions and start disappearing, that may indicate something is wrong in the environment.

HABITAT FIRST

If endangered animals are to survive in the wild, their natural habitats must be protected from damage. At the end of the nineteenth century some governments began defending habitats by creating national parks and other nature reserves that are protected from harmful human activities such as mining, logging, hunting, fishing and other ways natural resources are exploited. Park rangers play an important role in ensuring that people respect protected areas and do not undertake illegal activities.

But parks also need appropriate funding to ensure the survival of the wildlife that lives in the parks, protect the environment and restore habitat as needed. In Canada, under the Conservative government (2006–2015), major budget cuts were made to national parks in 2012, which impacted their parks' staff and ecological integrity.

A coal mine in northeastern BC has destroyed mountain caribou habitat.

The caribou is an iconic Canadian species. The animal is engraved on the Canadian quarter. But today many caribou herds are in trouble, mostly because of habitat loss.

WILD ENCOUNTER
The wolves and bison of Yellowstone

When my daughter, Elodie, was four, I took her to Yellowstone National Park in the wintertime. There she saw many wildlife species she had never encountered before: wolves, coyotes and bison. How lucky we are to enjoy this special place where animals can thrive. It constantly reminds me of the importance of protected areas for wildlife. In 1872 Yellowstone National Park became the world's first national park. The population of grizzly bears living there has gone from less than 150 in the 1970s to around 700 in 2017. That year President Trump removed the Yellowstone grizzly bears from the endangered species list. The decision to remove the special protections for this population of bears is opposed by a number of conservation groups who say it will leave the bears vulnerable to trophy hunters and may reverse decades of conservation efforts. They also say the bears are at risk from a diminishing food source and that climate change could impact the Yellowstone ecosystem and its wildlife.

Yellowstone is also the only place in the United States where bison have continuously lived since prehistoric times. Millions of bison once roamed the Great Plains. But the largest mammals in North America were hunted to near extinction in the 1800s. By 1889 there were fewer than 1,000 animals left. In 1902 there were only thirty. The United States Army protected the few wild bison remaining at Yellowstone from poachers. At the turn of the twentieth century a few conservationists, supported by former president Theodore Roosevelt, were able to rescue the bison from extinction. Now it's estimated that there are around 5,000 bison in Yellowstone.

One summer I was walking on the shoreline of a small island off the west coast of Vancouver Island in British Columbia. From the shore I noticed shiny black heads at the surface of the water. At first I thought they were part of the kelp plants, but when I looked with my binoculars, I realized it was a raft of about 120 sea otters. What a sight! I am always happy when I see sea otters in BC, because they were not always there. People used to hunt sea otters for their fur, and they were gone from British Columbia's waters by the 1930s. In the late 1960s and '70s, eighty-nine otters were reintroduced from Alaska to the west coast of Vancouver Island. They have since reproduced and are doing well. Biologists describe sea otters as a **keystone species**, meaning that as they come back they transform the environment around them. They are real eco-engineers, and their return has led to the rebirth of some habitats. When sea otters are gone from an area, sea urchins flourish and eat kelp beds. But when the otters move in, they devour the urchins, and kelp forests can grow again. Kelp forests provide shelter and food for many other species of invertebrates and fish, and they also help control carbon levels in the atmosphere. Sea otters remind us that each species plays a different role in the ecosystem. When you take one species out, it can impact the whole environment in unpredictable ways.

In the United States President Donald Trump has eliminated many environmental protection rules since taking office in 2017. He overturned a ban on the hunting of grizzly bears and wolves in Alaska wildlife refuges. He also opened new areas for offshore drilling, from the Atlantic to the Arctic Oceans, a move many environmental groups denounced as causing severe harm to the country's oceans and marine life. Trump has also permitted exploratory mining near national parks in zones where it was previously prohibited. In February 2018 his decision to scale back two national monuments in Utah took effect: Bears Ears National Monument was shrunk by 85 percent, and Grand Staircase-Escalante National Monument by half. These reductions—which conservation groups are challenging—mean that some of the land will now be open to mineral and oil and gas extraction.

These decisions pose a severe threat to dozens of fragile and endangered species, including the greater sage-grouse, an iconic bird that roams across eleven western states and two Canadian provinces. Once numbering in the millions,

Every spring greater sage-grouse males gather on "leks," or mating grounds, where they carry out their elaborate courtship displays.

In the spring shorebirds on their long migratory journey stop to feed and rest on the mud flats of Roberts Bank, near the mouth of the Fraser River in BC.

the bird has already lost nearly half its sagebrush habitat to development—to farms and ranches, to oil and gas operations, to spreading cities and lately to wind farms. Fire and invasive plants have also taken a toll.

Sometimes it is not enough to protect a specific area for wildlife, because animals move across several areas and migrate without paying attention to borders. As a result, conservation plans have to protect the travel corridors that connect different natural areas and consider all the different habitats species use during their life cycle.

For example, monarch butterflies undertake an extraordinary migration. Each fall as cold weather approaches, millions of butterflies leave Canada and the northern United States and begin flying south. They travel up to 2,800 miles (4,500 kilometers) until they reach Mexico, where they spend the winter. Because they have such a large range, they also encounter multiple threats. In Mexico they need forests in which to spend the winter, but some of the trees the butterflies use have been cut down to make way for human activities. In the United States and Canada, monarchs lay their eggs on a specific plant called milkweed. Once hatched the monarch larvae eat milkweed leaves. However, people have destroyed a lot of milkweed plants. So if they want to help butterflies, people have to look at solutions that protect what the butterflies need in all the different places that they visit.

Shorebirds also undertake great migrations, and because they travel thousands of miles per year, they encounter numerous threats along the way. Many populations of shorebirds have declined around the world. Scientists are now trying to understand what the biggest dangers are and how best to help shorebirds across the multiple habitats and countries they visit.

Each fall monarch butterflies set out on an incredible journey from the United States and Canada to their wintering sites in the mountain forests of Mexico, where they cluster together. Theirs is one of the world's longest insect migrations.

LAW AND ENFORCEMENT FOR WILDLIFE IN DANGER

Many countries have passed laws to protect certain species and habitats. Some *contaminants* and pesticides harmful to wildlife have been banned. But laws do not always work, especially if they are not enforced. In 1975 the Convention on Trade in Endangered Species of Wild Fauna and Flora was created to save species from overexploitation. So far 183 countries have signed the convention and have implemented laws to fight crimes against wildlife. However, the illegal killing of animals continues, including in national parks, as laws are not well enforced and countries lack the capacity to watch over large nature reserves. African great apes are protected by national and international laws, but people continue to hunt them illegally. In many countries, local conservation groups work with governments to catch poachers and patrol areas where the lives of animals such as rhinos and elephants are in danger. The job of park rangers who protect wildlife in the field is very dangerous. Many have lost their lives while fighting poachers.

Sometimes it takes the extraordinary will of an individual to save a species from extinction. In 1967 Dian Fossey moved from the United States and created the Karisoke Research Center in Rwanda's Virunga Mountains in Africa to study the mountain gorillas. She discovered that the gorillas were in great danger. Dian Fossey spent eighteen years studying the gorillas and fighting for their survival, organizing the first anti-poaching patrols in the area. She was murdered in 1985. To this day her murder remains unsolved. Thanks to Dian Fossey's work, mountain gorillas have been saved from extinction. Now the Dian Fossey Gorilla Fund continues to protect the animals and works with the local communities so that wildlife and people can thrive together.

Illegal hunting of hippos and trade in their teeth, along with habitat loss, climate change and conflicts with humans, are the greatest threats to hippos today.

WILD ENCOUNTER
Bald eagles, my neighbors

Bald eagles are part of my daily life. I often see them circling high in the sky when I look up from my garden on Salt Spring Island. As I admire them, I am grateful for the actions that conservationists took a few decades ago to save bald eagles. Bald eagles used to be hunted. They also suffered because of the pesticide DDT, which made the shells of eagles' eggs so weak that the eggs cracked in the nest before the chicks were ready to hatch. In 1940 the US Congress passed the Bald Eagle Protection Act, and in 1972 DDT was banned. More habitat was also protected. As a result of these actions, bald eagles started recovering. The bald eagle was among one of the first species to be protected by the Endangered Species Act, a law passed in 1973 in the United States to protect species at risk of extinction.

Wildlife biologist and conservationist David Hancock has been watching bald eagles in British Columbia for more than sixty-five years. In the early 1960s, as he flew over waterways and forest edges in his plane, he counted only three pairs of nesting eagles in British Columbia's Fraser Valley. At that time eagles were considered vermin: from 1917 to 1952, a bounty on bald eagles sponsored by the Alaska government eliminated at least 120,000 birds (killed in Washington State as well as in Alaska). David decided to dedicate his life and work to conserving bald eagles and changing public attitudes. Now he estimates there are 35,000 eagles alighting in the lower Fraser Valley as they pass through each year. This may be the largest bald eagle gathering in the world.

Juvenile burrowing owls represent hope for the recovery of the burrowing owl population in BC.

ACT FOR THE WILD

Bringing a tiny owl back

Burrowing owls may be tiny—the size of a can of pop—but they are fierce! They can imitate the hissing sound of a rattlesnake to discourage predators that are getting too close to their burrows. In British Columbia burrowing owls have been gone since 1980, mostly because their **grassland** habitat has been lost. In 1990 a group of volunteers who loved the owls got together and decided they would do everything they could to bring burrowing owls back to the areas where they had lived before. They started raising owls in captivity. The Burrowing Owl Conservation Society (BOCS) raises more than 100 owls every year that are released into the grasslands of the Okanagan. Initially wild owls from Washington State were used for breeding. BOCS has also built artificial burrows for the owls to nest in. This program takes a lot of effort, hope and commitment, and whether it will work in the long run is still unknown. But watching burrowing owls in their grasslands habitat is a magical experience.

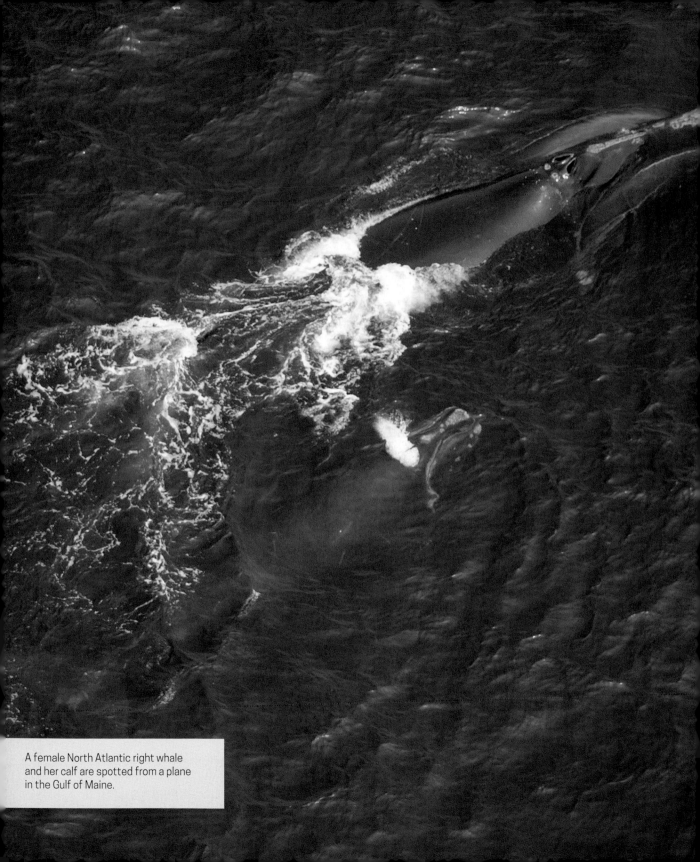

A female North Atlantic right whale and her calf are spotted from a plane in the Gulf of Maine.

ACT FOR THE WILD

Right-of-way for right whales

In 1992 a female North Atlantic right whale named Delilah was struck by a large ship in the Bay of Fundy. When she died, Delilah had a calf with her. Researchers did not think the calf would survive without a mother to guide her and no milk to help her grow, but she was so resourceful and independent that they decided to name her Calvin, after the adventurous little boy featured in the comic strip *Calvin and Hobbes*. In 2004 she had her first calf. Calvin's story became a symbol for the amazing ability of right whales to survive in a dangerous world.

Moira "Moe" Brown has studied the endangered North Atlantic right whale for over thirty years. When she realized that whales were being killed by ship strikes, Moe started working with the shipping industry to figure out how vessels and whales could coexist in Canadian waters. Because she had spent years studying the population, she knew exactly where the whales were. She convinced the shipping industry to change the shipping lanes in the Bay of Fundy in 2003. The changes reduced the chance that a ship would collide with a whale by 90 percent. In 2008 another area important to the whales, Roseway Basin, was further designated as an "area to be avoided." Moe's work made a difference for the whales but is not finished. When a number of whales moved to the Gulf of St. Lawrence, more rules were needed to avoid collisions between whales and ships.

CAPTIVE BREEDING FOR SPECIES ON THE BRINK

Sometimes a species can become so threatened that scientists have to step in to breed the animals in captivity and then return them to the wild.

The California condor is one of the largest flying birds in the world. It is striking, with its pink head and neck, black wings and amazing eyesight. The condor population was almost wiped out because of habitat destruction, poaching and poisoning. There were only twenty-two birds left in the wild in the 1980s, and wildlife scientists decided to start a *captive breeding* program to help the condors. Captive-bred condors are now released into the wild in California, Arizona and Mexico. Captive breeding is hard work, and often it is not enough if the birds, once released, are not safe in the wild. Scientists demonstrated that the biggest threat to condors was lead poisoning. When animals such as deer are shot by hunters with lead bullets, the condors who eat the carcasses also ingest the bullets, which poison and kill them. In 2013 California protected the condors by banning the use of lead ammunition.

The golden lion tamarin, a monkey that lives in Brazil's Atlantic Forest, was once in danger of extinction because of the destruction of the forest. The monkeys were often captured to be sold as pets. In order to save the species from extinction, scientists decided to raise the monkeys in captivity. To make sure the animals are safe once they are released into the wild in Brazil, actions have been taken to restore and protect the tamarins' natural habitat.

The California condor is the largest land bird in North America. Its wings span an amazing 9 to 10 feet (2 to 3 meters).
FRAYN/SHUTTERSTOCK.COM

Wildlife biologist David Hancock holds a juvenile bald eagle that is part of a tracking study to learn about eagles' movements.

A juvenile Oregon spotted frog is about to be released in a wetland.

ACT FOR THE WILD

A new home for Oregon spotted frogs

One spring I took Emile and Elodie to a special event: the release of 100 juvenile Oregon spotted frogs in a wetland in the Fraser Valley in British Columbia. Baby frogs are raised in captivity and released to increase the small existing populations in the wild. This wetland used to have frogs in the past, but the habitat had changed so much that they could no longer live there. The biologists wanted to give back the habitat to the frogs, so they repaired the wetland. In 2016, for the first time, they found Oregon spotted frog egg masses there, an exciting discovery. It meant that the released frogs were surviving and reproducing in the wild. Emile and Elodie had a chance to hold the frogs and watch them hop off their hands into their new home.

Public education and outreach are important components of western painted turtle recovery.

The western painted turtle is one of four recognized subspecies of painted turtles in North America, and it is British Columbia's only remaining native freshwater turtle, as another species, the western pond turtle, was *extirpated* (no longer exists in a specified geographic area but still exists elsewhere). The western painted turtle is listed as endangered because of major population declines due to habitat loss and fragmentation, road death, human disturbance, poaching, predation and invasive species. Western painted turtles are true masters of survival and have unique adaptations that help them withstand the harshest conditions. For example, in September baby turtles break out of their eggs but will stay in their shallow nest during the freezing winter. The tiny hatchlings possess a natural antifreeze and produce special proteins that cause ice crystals to form outside cells, preventing damage to tissue. When the weather warms up in the spring, they emerge intact.

A baby western painted turtle is released into a wetland in the Fraser Valley, BC.

But today, even with their exceptional ability to survive, western painted turtles are struggling in the modern world. As their habitat shrinks, turtles may choose nesting sites where their eggs are not able to survive, such as near campsites, swimming beaches, boat launches or in agricultural fields. In those areas the shallow nests are often accidentally dug up by people and dogs or destroyed by boats and trucks.

In 2012 eggs that were laid in two unsafe nests were collected for the first time to test whether it was possible to raise western painted turtles in captivity. A year later twelve baby turtles were released at the same lakes where they were first gathered. Since then turtles are raised in captivity and released every year to help regrow the wild populations.

FIGHTING THE INVADERS

The Action Plan for Australian Mammals 2012 reviewed the conservation status of all Australian mammals and identified predation by the introduced domestic cat and the European red fox as having had the most detrimental impact on *terrestrial* mammal species. The Australian Wildlife Conservancy is conducting several programs to try to reduce the impact of cats. One of them is the establishment of large areas free of feral animals areas surrounded by conservation fences to protect native mammals. In other parts of the world, steps are also being taken to protect endangered native species against invasive predators.

Western painted turtles are vulnerable to road traffic near their nesting sites.

Nowhere Else on Earth: The Galapagos Islands

The Galapagos Islands are world famous as a laboratory of biological evolution. Many of the plants, birds and reptiles there are found nowhere else on earth. The islands are home to the world's only flightless cormorant. This bird, as well as many other species that live there, cannot defend itself against animals that people have brought to the islands, such as rats and cats. Since the 1980s conservation managers have removed invasive species in the Galapagos Islands to give the native wildlife a chance to thrive.

Giant tortoises have been in trouble for a long time in the Galapagos. In the late 1950s researchers discovered that only eleven of the fourteen original giant tortoise populations in the Galapagos still existed. Almost all of them were close to extinction. In the two centuries prior, sailors, pirates and merchants had killed many giant tortoises on the islands. They had taken the tortoises for food and also for their oil, which was used for everything from heating to cosmetics. Humans also brought animals to the islands, such as rats, pigs, and goats, that killed the tortoise eggs and hatchlings or destroyed their habitat. After Galapagos National Park was established in 1959, park guards put an end to the killing of tortoises for food. Biologists from the Charles Darwin Research Station developed a plan to help them. In order to save giant tortoises from extinction, some of the reptiles were taken into captivity, and a captive breeding program began. One species, the Pinzon Island tortoise, had a big problem because black rats were eating all its babies. In the 1960s the park guards started removing eggs from tortoise nests, raising the hatchlings in captivity and then releasing the tortoises back into the wild once they were big enough that rats could not hurt them.

Project Isabela, initiated in 1997, eliminated more than 140,000 feral goats over a decade on Pinta, Santiago and Isabela Islands. In 2012 all black rats were removed from Pinzon Island so that new tortoise hatchlings could survive

The flightless cormorant is found only on the Galapagos Islands. Pairs perform a unique courtship dance that involves them intertwining their necks.

and complete their life cycle. At the same time, conservation managers restored the habitat on some of the islands. Now when tortoises are released back into the wild, it is a much safer environment for them. Following the rat elimination, giant tortoise hatchlings were encountered on Pinzon island for the first time in over 100 years.

Lonesome George was born on the Galapagos Islands. He was a male Pinta Island tortoise and the last known individual of the subspecies. In his last years George was known as the rarest creature in the world. He lived at the Charles Darwin Research Station, and for years scientists tried to get the giant tortoise to find a mate, but they were

Galapagos tortoises are herbivorous, feeding primarily on cactus pads, grasses and native fruits. They move large quantities of seeds over long distances.

It is quite common to see tiny birds such as finches and vermilion flycatchers perched on top of Galapagos tortoises. These birds have developed a special relationship with the tortoises, feeding on the insects that hide in the folds of the tortoises' skin or shell.

unsuccessful. In the 1990s they brought over two female tortoises, from Wolf Volcano on northern Isabela Island, that seemed most similar to Pinta tortoises. Unfortunately, Lonesome George showed no interest in his new companions. Later on scientists discovered that Pinta tortoises are most closely related to the Española tortoise. George then shared his enclosure with two female Españolas, but he never produced any offspring. Teams searched the world's zoos and private collections for another Pinta tortoise. None was ever found. Lonesome George was really alone. When he died in 2012, he was more than 100 years old. In the last few years, scientists studying the genetics of Galapagos giant tortoises have occasionally found hybrid tortoises, living on Wolf Volcano on northern Isabela Island, that have half or less Pinta ancestry. The scientists hope that these hybrids could one day help in the plan to restore tortoises to Pinta Island. The Galapagos Conservancy and the Galapagos National Park Directorate work together on the Giant Tortoise Restoration Initiative to restore tortoise populations across the Galapagos Islands.

The death of Lonesome George reminds us of the crisis turtles are in today. (The word *turtle* refers to all animals with a bony shell and a backbone that belong to the order Testudines, which includes turtles, tortoises and terrapins. Tortoises live on land, while turtles can be aquatic, semi-aquatic or mostly terrestrial.) They have been around for more than 200 million years, even outliving the dinosaurs, which disappeared over 65 million years ago. But today they are struggling to persist in a world dominated by their worst enemy: humans. According to a study published in 2018 by researchers from the University of Georgia, the University of California-Davis, the US Geological Survey and the Tennessee

Aquarium Conservation Institute, of the 356 species of turtles worldwide, approximately 61 percent are threatened or already extinct. Turtles are among the most threatened of the major groups of vertebrates, more so than birds, mammals, fishes or even amphibians. Turtles are in crisis because of habitat loss, poaching, the pet trade and climate change. When we lose turtles, we also lose the powerful benefits they provide to ecosystems. Turtles play an important role: they disperse seeds, open paths in dense vegetation, create habitat for other species and maintain healthy food webs.

THE LAST CHANCE

In some cases so few animals are left in the wild that people have to take extreme actions to try to save some species from extinction. Unfortunately it does not always work. Here are some examples, some more successful than others.

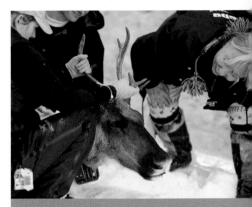

An Indigenous Elder comforts a female caribou before it is temporarily placed in a pen to protect it from predators.

Vaquita: The Panda of the Sea

The vaquita is the smallest and also the rarest marine mammal in the world. It is known as the "panda of the sea" because of the distinctive markings that circle its eyes. This tiny porpoise lives only in the Gulf of California near Mexico. Over the years many vaquitas died from being caught accidentally in fishing nets. The situation is so serious that scientists estimate that in 2018, there may be only fifteen animals left. In 2005 the Mexican government banned the use of gillnets, the fishing nets that are dangerous to the vaquita. At the same time a conservation group started to work with the Mexican Navy to enforce the law and stop illegal fishing. But it was not enough. In a final attempt to save the vaquita, scientists tried to capture the last vaquitas. They wanted to move them to a safe space where they would be

Whooping-crane chicks born in captivity are raised by staff who wear full-length crane costumes to make sure the cranes imprint on whooping cranes rather than humans. The costume and hand puppet mimic the colors and shape of an adult bird. Imprinting refers to a critical time early in an animal's life when it forms social bonds and develops a concept of its own identity. If young birds imprint on people instead of becoming attached to their own parents, this may decrease their ability to live in the wild and have relationships with their own species.

protected from the dangerous fishing activities and have a chance to recover. Unfortunately, the rescue operation was not successful, and now more work has to be done to protect the porpoises.

Whooping Crane: The Tallest Bird in North America

In 1941 there were only sixteen whooping cranes left in the world. This large bird—the tallest in North America— almost went extinct because of hunting and habitat loss. People started raising birds in captivity and releasing them in the wild. That was not easy. Whooping cranes are migratory birds. In nature, the young ones follow their parents on their first flight and learn the route as they go. But birds born in captivity have to be taught by humans. Pilots used ultralight planes to guide young whooping cranes along a migration route from Wisconsin to Florida in what became known as Operation Migration. Many people became captivated by the birds' adventures and followed the migration path on maps. It was one of the most well-known, beloved and unexpected conservation efforts in North America, even though the results were mixed.

Advanced Technologies to the Rescue

A long time ago rhinos roamed across Africa's savanna and Asia's tropical forests. But today all five species of rhino are in trouble because of habitat loss and poaching for rhino horns. Sudan was the last male of his subspecies. When the forty-five-year-old northern white rhino died in March 2018 in Kenya, his plight drew international attention to rhinoceros conservation and to the huge worldwide loss of species. Northern white rhinoceroses used to be found in an area including Uganda, Chad, southwestern Sudan, the Central

African Republic and the Democratic Republic of the Congo. War and poaching drove them to extinction. Sudan lived in the Ol Pejeta Conservancy, along with the last two northern white rhino females, named Najin and Fatu.

Scientists are now doing everything they can to try to keep northern white rhinos from disappearing entirely. They are developing advanced reproductive techniques, including in vitro fertilization to create northern white rhino embryos that could be carried by female southern white rhinos, a related subspecies that still exists in the wild.

The white rhinoceros is the largest species of land mammal after the elephant. There are two distinct subspecies, but only the southern white rhino still exists in the wild, the majority in just four countries: South Africa, Namibia, Zimbabwe and Kenya. Poaching for the illegal trade in their horns is the major threat to rhinos.

A pair of Laysan ducks in Midway Atoll National Wildlife Refuge.

ACT FOR THE WILD

Don't put all your ducks in one basket

The critically endangered Laysan duck is one of the rarest ducks in the world, with one of the smallest geographic ranges of any duck species. Laysan ducks once lived on several of the Hawaiian Islands but started disappearing with the arrival of invasive rats. The last birds were found on Laysan Island, a single tiny island almost 1,000 miles (1,600 kilometers) from Oahu.

When humans introduced rabbits to this island, the duck population was almost destroyed. By 1911 there were only eleven ducks left. After the rabbits were eliminated from the island, the ducks started recovering. But with all the birds living on a single island, they were at risk: if something were to happen—such as a natural disaster, the arrival of a predator or a disease outbreak—the entire species could be wiped out forever. Because the ducks do not fly between the atolls, they needed some help.

The US Fish and Wildlife Service decided that the duck's best chance for survival was to create an additional population on another island. In 2004 and 2005 forty-two ducks were moved to Sand and Eastern Islands in Midway Atoll, and soon new ducklings were born on the islands. Before getting the ducks to their new homes, the biologists prepared the islands and restored the habitat so the birds could nest. The project was successful, and the two populations had grown to almost 1,000 birds when a tsunami hit the islands in 2011. Many birds died. In 2014 twenty-eight Laysan ducks were moved to Kure Atoll to create a third population. The ducks remain vulnerable to extinction because of climate change: with rising sea levels, the low-lying islands where the ducks live could become flooded. This is why at least two additional populations need to occur. One of those sites should be an island that is large and high enough to withstand climate change and sea-level rise.

Woodland caribou roam a mountaintop in the South Peace region of BC.

ACT FOR THE WILD

Saving caribou, one animal at a time

On a sunny day in March I was in a helicopter flying over the snow-covered mountains of northern British Columbia with a wildlife biologist. We were looking for the last herds of mountain woodland caribou. I had always wanted to see caribou. To me they symbolize the vast Canadian wilderness. They have been on the Canadian quarter since 1936. But now most of the caribou herds in Canada are in trouble. In the area we were flying over, human activities such as logging and mining have destroyed a lot of the caribou's habitat. Many herds are down to only a few animals. We finally spotted five or six caribou that were gracefully moving on the mountaintops. The males with their antlers were majestic. We followed them for a while until they stopped at the edge of the mountain: a coal mine was in front of them. It was very sad to see.

But in this area the local First Nations communities decided to help the last animals before they disappeared forever. They captured some pregnant females and placed them in a pen that they guarded day and night from wolves and bears. Once the caribou gave birth and the calves were strong enough, the animals were returned to the wild, to areas where they had a better chance of withstanding wolf predation. Caribou and predators have coexisted on the landscape for a long time. However, as humans have claimed land for logging, oil and gas exploration and coal mining, caribou have less and less habitat in which to roam and stay safe. Clear-cuts have produced an environment more favorable to species such as moose and deer. Those animals in turn have attracted wolves. Caribou didn't encounter wolves much in the past, but now the wolves travel into previously inaccessible caribou country along the roads, pipelines and seismic lines (narrow trails used in oil and gas exploration) created by humans. Until habitat is returned to caribou and development stops, caribou will have a hard time surviving. If not for the commitment of a few local people doing everything they can for the survival of the wildlife they love, these animals would no longer exist.

Some people criticize these new hi-tech solutions to save species from extinction and say more should be done to protect rhinos in the wild instead. Others believe that these extreme solutions are needed because the northern white rhino will become extinct otherwise.

Protecting the Future of Hawaii's Native Plants

Hawaii is a hot spot for unique plants found nowhere else in the world. Unfortunately, the flora there is so threatened that Hawaii has come to be known as the "endangered species capital of the world," with nearly 40 percent of all endangered plants in the United States. The Plant Extinction Prevention Program (PEPP) works to protect Hawaii's rarest and endangered plant species. It focuses on the 237 plant species that have fewer than fifty plants in the wild, which means they are at imminent risk of extinction. One of the biggest threats to the plants on the Hawaiian Islands is the damage caused by introduced animals such as pigs, goats, deer and cattle. When plants disappear, it creates cascading effects: the plant pollinators also disappear, which results in more plants vanishing, which leaves less fruit for native birds. Bird populations decline and as a result have fewer opportunities to carry plant seeds to new places, which weakens plants even more. The people working for PEPP protect the plants from being trampled by introduced animals. They control small predators such as rodents and remove the non-native plants. They also collect fruit, seeds, cuttings and pollen from plants in the field to preserve them so they could recover the species if they were to become extirpated.

Cattle grazing can have a damaging impact on local ecosystems, vegetation and soil quality and can also indirectly affect birds by removing shrubs that serve as bird habitat.

The Hawaiian silversword—known by its Hawaiian name ahinahina—is a threatened plant found in Haleakalā National Park, on the island of Maui. It almost became extinct because of animal grazing and visitors taking away the plants as souvenirs. Protection measures have since helped this unique species recover. PUNG/SHUTTERSTOCK.COM

ACT FOR THE WILD

Dogs and people working together to save cheetahs

In the 1970s a young American woman named Laurie Marker visited Namibia. She discovered that farmers there were killing cheetahs because they thought the cats were eating their goats and sheep. Laurie became worried about the survival of cheetahs, the fastest land animals on earth. She realized that nobody was doing anything to help the cheetahs, so she decided to move to Namibia and find solutions herself. Laurie knew it was important to work with the local farmers, and she went to visit them at their houses. She wanted to find a way for the cheetahs and the farmers to live together peacefully on the same land, and she got dogs to help her with that.

Since 1994 the organization Laurie created in 1990, the Cheetah Conservation Fund, has been placing Anatolian shepherd and Kangal dogs on farms in Namibia to protect livestock against predators. The program works! Livestock losses have been reduced by 80 to 100 percent on farms with guard dogs, and now many farmers do not see the cheetah as an enemy.

When I visited Laurie, the dogs and the cheetahs in Namibia, I took Elodie with me. It was her first time in Africa—she was fourteen years old—and she did not know much about cheetahs. After seeing all the work Laurie did with the local people to keep cheetahs safe in the country, Elodie was inspired. Laurie's passion and dedication for cheetahs is contagious. When you meet her, you immediately want to help. Elodie was surprised to meet so many young people from all over the world who had traveled to Namibia to help Laurie and the cheetahs. She realized that everybody can help, no matter how old they are. Elodie has already asked me if she can go back as a volunteer soon.

Cheetah keeper Becky Johnston attends to the cheetahs' morning run at the Cheetah Conservation Fund in Otjiwarongo, Namibia.

Northern red-legged frogs are found throughout the Pacific Northwest. They are greatly impacted by habitat loss and degradation, as well as predation by and competition from introduced amphibians and fish.

4

ENDANGERED SPECIES IN YOUR BACKYARD

Many species are declining, and you may wonder what you can do to change that. The problems affecting wildlife are not always easy to solve. However, each of us can take action before it is too late. Saving any animal or ecosystem begins with an individual person. Everyone, regardless of age, can do something to help. In all corners of the world people are becoming more aware that species are in trouble and are working hard to save them in different ways. Kids can help too, and they do not have to travel to the far side of the world to help protect endangered wildlife. Conservation starts right in your backyard. Keep your eyes and ears open, look into a pond, look up in the sky, take notice of the life around you, and you will find your own way to help. Whatever action you take will add to actions other kids are taking elsewhere to help endangered wildlife.

HABITAT FOR WILDLIFE

One of the most important ways you can help plants and animals is to protect their habitat. Learn about the species that live near you. Connect with a local group that helps protect or restore habitat for these species. You might help remove invasive plants that compete with native species in a wetland, or help plant local vegetation that will provide better habitat for wildlife.

If you live in a house with a garden, you can help animals by creating wildlife-friendly habitat in your own backyard. Plant a variety of native flowers, grasses, trees and shrubs, and your garden can become a nature reserve that birds, bees and butterflies will use for food, shelter and nesting. Make sure to have local plants that flower at different times of the year to support pollinators. Don't use pesticides, which are harmful to wildlife. Make frogs and salamanders happy by building a pond for them where they can lay eggs. Many small mammals and amphibians use woody structures such as logs and stumps to hibernate in the winter. Ask your parents not to remove larger trees, stumps and logs from the property, as they are part of wildlife habitat!

Install bird feeders, and don't forget to clean them on a regular basis to protect the health of the birds that visit them. Put out a bird bath. Birds love water! Keep your cat indoors, since cats hunt and kill birds and other native wildlife. You can also install bat and bird boxes. Research what makes a good nest box for the species you are trying to attract: the size of the box and the entrance hole, the positioning and the materials you use are all important!

The chestnut-backed chickadee is a frequent visitor to backyard bird feeders.

Watch life unfold in front of your eyes, and take note of the different species that visit your garden.

You don't have to have a garden to make a difference. If you live in the city in an apartment with a balcony or a small outdoor space, you can work with your parents to place a few pots filled with native flowers to provide a food source for bees and butterflies. Local organizations such as community centers and gardening and birding groups often offer free information sessions on how to attract more birds, butterflies and bees to your outdoor space. You can learn about the right wildflower seeds to select for the abundant nectar their flowers produce. These attract both native and migratory birds and insects to your space

Elodie plants aquatic native plants in a wetland in the Fraser Valley of BC.

to fuel up naturally, and you can even achieve this with containers on your balcony.

You can also support parks in the city you live in. Urban parks are a great way to learn more about the natural world. They often have conservation programs for kids and may even offer a safe haven for species at risk in the urban environment. In Vancouver, British Columbia, Stanley Park has one of the largest urban colonies of Pacific great blue herons in North America. Pacific great blue herons are considered a species at risk in Canada, their populations declining because of habitat loss and human disturbance. Seeing these magnificent birds in and around the park is always a special experience. In the summer of 2018 there were eighty-five active heron nests with ninety-eight *fledglings*

A great blue heron in Stanley Park in Vancouver, BC. Herons return to the colony in February and March. Males are often the first to return to claim the best nests.

(baby birds old enough to learn to fly). The Stanley Park Ecology Society monitors the heronry and also runs education programs, restores habitat for wildlife, manages invasive species and more. The society always welcomes volunteers to help monitor birds, remove invasive species or engage park visitors with information about the natural world to spread the joy of connecting with nature. Find out more about parks in your city and what they do to support biodiversity.

Watch That Hummingbird: We Are All Connected!

When you watch a hummingbird visit a feeder, a window opens on a larger world. When I see the brilliantly colored rufous hummingbird at our feeder on Salt Spring Island in the spring, I think about the fact that this tiny bird undertakes an impressive migratory journey from Alaska to Mexico.

BECOME A CITIZEN SCIENTIST

Scientists need to obtain knowledge about species so they can better protect them. Wildlife populations are dynamic, and scientists cannot always document the complex movements and distribution of all species, so they rely on volunteers to help them collect data through *citizen science*. Learning how to identify species is the first step toward taking conservation action. You can join a local nature club, where you will develop your identification skills, participate in surveys and monitor wildlife. At first you may find it daunting to tell birds apart or figure out the difference between the egg masses of several amphibian species in a pond, but you will learn quickly. Everyone can participate in programs such as the Christmas Bird Count and the Great Backyard Bird Count. From anywhere in the world, you simply count the numbers and kinds of birds you see and submit the information for scientists to use.

A well-located hummingbird feeder in your garden will attract several visits a day. Make sure you frequently clean the feeder with hot tap water.

A barn swallow feeds an insect it just caught to its hungry nestlings. Both parents take care of the young.

ACT FOR THE WILD

Where have all the barn swallows gone?

My mother used to predict the weather by looking at the flight patterns of barn swallows (*hirondelles* in French). "Low flies the swallow, rain to follow," she would say. I grew up with the hirondelles in the South of France, and I remember the excitement we felt when we spotted a small nest under the roof of our house. I loved listening to the high-pitched sounds the swallows made during the warm summer nights. More than thirty years later, I look for the swallows every time I return to my parents' house. Sadly, I now stare at empty skies. The swallows are gone. The barn swallow is one of the world's most common bird species. Yet for decades now barn swallows, along with other birds that feed on flying insects, have been declining at an alarming rate. Scientists are still trying to understand why barn swallows are disappearing but suspect the reasons include a shortage of the flying insects they eat and the loss of nest sites.

You can help barn swallows by monitoring their nests near you and reporting your observations. NestWatch projects in Canada and the United States collect data on nesting birds. Nest monitoring provides information on the health of birds, how populations are changing over time and the impacts of human activities on birds. When we understand more about why a species is in decline, we can more effectively take actions to protect it.

You can even observe birds at your feeders and send your sightings to Project FeederWatch. Scientists use the data coming from volunteers to better understand bird populations, identify declines and learn about the impacts of climate change, urban development, agriculture and more.

REDUCE YOUR IMPACT ON YOUR ENVIRONMENT

You can help protect endangered wildlife by changing some things about the way you live.

• Buy and use less stuff, and reuse and recycle as much as you can. If you have old books, toys or clothes in good condition that you don't want, give them to a charity instead of throwing them away. When you recycle you cut down on pollution, but you also help wildlife by preserving their natural habitats.

• Be aware of how much plastic you use. When you buy something avoid unnecessary packaging, and remember to bring your own shopping bags. Avoid buying bottled water. Drink tap water from a glass or a reusable drink container. Water bottles, plastic bags and other debris end up in lakes and oceans and are found in the stomachs of many animals, including whales, sea turtles and seabirds. As the amount of sea trash increases, so do the risks to marine life. Today the presence of plastics in the seas and oceans is one of the greatest threats to wildlife throughout the world. Help create change by making a conscious choice to use less plastic.

• Every year environmental groups organize the cleanup of local ponds, parks and seashores. It's a great way to help wildlife and the environment, and you will be surprised and shocked by how much garbage is out there.

• Think twice about the food you buy. Talk to your parents about buying locally grown produce. Transporting

On Florida's Atlantic coast, a researcher retrieves a balloon from the ocean after Valentine's Day. Balloons are dangerous to marine wildlife, which may mistake them for food and eat them.

food over long distances contributes to pollution. Try to avoid food treated with pesticides and eat organic food if possible. Cut down on meat. Look for products produced in a socially and environmentally responsible way (look for the Fair Trade label). Palm-oil trees grow in tropical rainforests. The clearing of these forests for conventional palm-oil plantations has destroyed the habitat of endangered species such as orangutans, tigers, elephants and rhinos. In Borneo the critically endangered orangutan population has experienced a dramatic decline. Nearly 150,000 animals have been lost from the island's forests in the last sixteen years. The greatest losses have occurred in regions where the forest has been cut down to make way for palm-oil plantations. You can help by buying only products made with certified sustainable palm oil.

• Learn about the fish you eat and choose only seafood that is fished or farmed in ways that have minimal impact on the environment. Programs such as Ocean Wise and the Monterey Bay Aquarium Seafood Watch can help you make the right choices for healthy oceans.

• When you are on holiday, be aware that many tourist products, such ivory, tortoiseshell, coral and fur, are made from threatened species. Do not buy or release exotic animals—they are not meant to be pets.

Wilderness Committee members at the legislature in Victoria, BC, deliver a petition, signed by more than 40,000 people, calling for legislation to protect endangered species.

BE A VOICE FOR THE VOICELESS

You can contribute toward a better future for endangered species by raising awareness around you. Knowledge of a problem is the first step toward taking action and finding solutions. Share what you learn with others. Maybe your favorite species is elephants or polar bears or a salamander that lives near you. Maybe you are concerned about a natural

An orphaned harbor seal pup is rehabilitated at the Vancouver Aquarium's Marine Mammal Rescue Centre. Once the pup is healthy again, it will be returned to the wild.

area that is at risk of being destroyed. Make your voice heard, and spread the word. Write a letter to your local newspaper or a poem to be shared at school. Shoot a video clip and share it on social media. Write a letter to government officials, explaining your concerns and asking them to make changes. Sign a petition to demand a change in the law, and share it with others. Talk to your friends and family about the issue so that as many people as possible can become informed and act. Join others and attend environmental rallies.

Make Art for Endangered Species

Art allows us to appreciate the world around us in a unique way. Art speaks to our hearts and can play an important role in inspiring people to protect the natural world. Choose your favorite threatened species and draw a picture, make a sculpture, create a mask or make a short animated film about it. I have worked in schools with many students and their teachers who have used art as a tool to inspire people to take action for the protection of endangered species. You can do it too!

Opening night for an exhibition in Vancouver, BC, featuring artwork created by children to inspire people to protect BC's endangered species. Photo Michael Wheatley.

Volunteer for a Cause

Conservation organizations around the world rely on volunteers to help them protect endangered species. Find the cause that speaks to your heart and research a volunteer program you can sign up for. Are you concerned about rhinoceros poaching in Africa? You can volunteer for a group dedicated to rhino conservation and help monitor populations. Or you can volunteer for a program that rescues animals that have been injured in the wild.

You don't have to go to Africa to help the rhinoceros. Every year the International Rhino Foundation engages everyone—kids and adults, wherever they live—to join them

A student is releasing a bird as part of an educational banding program near Vancouver, BC.

to celebrate the "Cinco de Rhino" on May 5. During this one day the foundation raises funds for rhino conservation and tries to get people around the world talking about the importance of protecting endangered rhinos and their habitats. Throw a party with friends, share fun facts, run your own fundraising campaign to support research and conservation of the world's rhino species, or simply help raise awareness. The foundation's website has a party toolkit and rhino fact sheets that you can download to get you started. It is easy to join Team Rhino, and it can make a difference! Many other conservation organizations have similar initiatives. Just find the cause that speaks to your heart!

You don't have to travel far from where you live to find an organization that makes a difference. Contact a group and let them know you would really like to help out. Wherever you live, there will be wildlife or a special place that needs your protection. You can join a young naturalists club and be part of such activities as building bat boxes or monitoring a local marsh. Many groups will allow you to "adopt" an endangered animal to help support their campaigns. They will send you an adoption certificate and photograph of the animal you have helped sponsor. You can organize a garage sale or sell homemade cookies in your school and neighborhood, and give the money to a group working on conservation activities. Use social media to raise awareness about endangered species, and encourage others to join you.

GO OUTSIDE AND ENJOY NATURE!

Visit local nature reserves, national parks and wildlife projects near your home and while on vacation. Your support helps them survive and will also remind you why it is so important to protect natural habitats and species. Parks often have special guided tours and walks for kids. Talk to the naturalists about the threatened species in the area, how they are being protected and how you might be able to help. When you visit a nature park, make sure you respect the environment and the wildlife. Follow regulations, keep dogs on leash, do not take anything, and put your rubbish in a bin or take it with you.

Support Responsible Wildlife Watching

Do not support activities in nature that exploit wildlife. Do not ride on an elephant's back, do not participate in "swim with dolphins" programs, and don't go to shows that exhibit captive animals for entertainment. In many parts of the world, animals are forced to perform tricks in front of tourists. There are many examples: terrified orangutans fighting with boxing gloves strapped to their wrists in Thailand; elephants dancing or giving rides to tourists; dolphins performing shows every day in aquariums such as SeaWorld. Performing animals are often illegally taken from the wild and traded for use in these shows. Cruelty becomes part of their everyday lives. They are beaten, their spirits are broken by handlers, and they often live in barren enclosures. Whales, dolphins and porpoises suffer physically and mentally from life in captivity in aquariums.

Slow down, look closely, and take the time to observe sea life in tide pools. Creatures blend into their environment, so be patient and you will find treasures.

Make the right choice: do not visit these shows, no matter how much you want to see the animals. Instead, visit the websites of organizations such as the Born Free Foundation or the Brigitte Bardot Foundation and learn how you can support campaigns against the exploitation of wild animals in captivity.

LOOKING TO THE FUTURE: DON'T GIVE UP!

Every time I am out for a walk on my own or with my children, I take notice of the wildlife around me, and I encourage my children to do the same. It can be as simple as noticing a hummingbird when it visits my balcony in downtown Vancouver, watching a great blue heron fishing on the seawall, not far from people who are out for a run or a bike ride, or admiring a bald eagle perching on a tall tree near the beach. What a gift to us! These sights inspire and enrich my heart and soul. But I also remember how vulnerable these species are. Their quiet hardships can easily go unnoticed, and when I think of the possibility of losing these—or any—species, I feel truly devastated. Can you imagine what that would be like? Empty skies and oceans, no birdsong or frog sounds? Is that the world we want? In our busy lives we try so hard to keep our distance from the natural world, but we are in this together: we are part of nature, and nature is part of us. It is our responsibility to protect wild animals and wild places. Our future depends on it.

When you learn about the thousands of species that are in trouble in the world, you may feel sad and powerless. Fixing problems takes time, and if you quit too soon the species you care about might lose out. Luckily there are many amazing people around the world who have dedicated their lives to fighting the war against extinction. But more people and more action are needed. All of us can help and be good stewards of our shared planet, raising awareness and inspiring others to do more.

Every single action counts. It is important to start acting now. Your passion, commitment and care can make a difference in the world you live in. Remember that you are not alone and that together we can save precious species before they are gone forever!

Enjoy nature in your backyard. Get a pair of binoculars to observe birds, and learn how to identify them.

Elodie connects with a barn owl she has just learned to band.

ACT FOR THE WILD

Elise and the badger

Solitary and shy, American badgers live in big burrows. Known for their large and powerful paws, badgers can dig at the rate of three feet (one meter) a minute in search of prey. They are also very fragile. In southern British Columbia they are losing the grasslands where they live, they are killed by cars when they cross the highway, and they are also persecuted by people who don't understand them. I once spent two full days in the same spot, waiting for a badger to come out of its burrow. Finally a badger made an appearance, and it was worth waiting for. A few months later an eleven-year old girl named Elise saw our badger images and footage, and she fell in love with the badgers. She realized that badgers were in trouble, and although she had never seen them in the wild, she wanted to do something to help them. She made connections with the Wilderness Committee, an environmental group. She found out that British Columbia did not have any law to protect endangered species such as the badger and that the Wilderness Committee had a petition calling for a change. Elise signed the petition right away and decided she wanted to do more. After school she knocked on her neighbors' doors and went to the local dog park to talk to people about the plight of British Columbia's endangered species. At first it was difficult and awkward for Elise to approach people she did not know. She was not sure if anyone cared or would listen to her. But she did not give up, and over five months she gathered more than 800 signatures on her petition calling for an endangered species law. In February 2017 the Wilderness Committee delivered 40,090 petition signatures calling for provincial endangered species legislation to the BC Legislature.

An American badger makes a rare appearance in front of its burrow.

2010 BROKEN PROMISE
STOP THE SCAR!
WWW.EAGLERIDGEBLUFFS.CA

Elodie on the scene of a local environmental protest.

ACT FOR THE WILD

Stop, don't break the mountain!

On Easter Monday in 2006 twenty Canadians grabbed their camping gear and left their homes to build a tent city at Eagleridge Bluffs, an area in West Vancouver, British Columbia. They were protesting the government's plan to build a highway through the bluffs. The highway expansion was meant to improve the road between Vancouver and Whistler in preparation for the 2010 Olympic Winter Games. The protesters argued that it would destroy sensitive ecosystems. The northern red-legged frog, listed as a species of special concern in BC, also inhabits this area. The protesters had written letters, organized community rallies and spoken to people at different levels of government to try to stop the project. But when they realized they were not being heard, they camped on the site for forty days to stop highway contractors from cutting trees and clearing the land.

They were not successful, but they set an example and inspired many of the kids who were part of the protest. Elodie was three years old when she camped on the bluffs with her father. It was her first environmental protest, and when I asked her what she understood of the protest, she said, "Stop, don't break the mountain!" During this time Elodie and the other kids met a 78-year-old veteran activist named Betty Krawczyk, who shared many stories of protesting against the logging of old-growth forest. The children were captivated. Environmental rallies like this bring together people of all ages and from all walks of life. When you stand up to save an endangered species or its habitat, you can meet new friends. You don't have to do it all alone!

GLOSSARY

amphibian—a class of vertebrate (having a spine) organisms that includes frogs, toads, newts and salamanders; most amphibians are born in water and breathe with gills, then transform into adults that live mostly on land and breathe through lungs

apes—large primates that lack a tail, including the gorilla, chimpanzee, orangutan and gibbon

biodiversity—the variety of life in a geographic region or ecosystem; an area with many different kinds of plants and animals is said to have high biodiversity, indicating a healthy ecosystem

bushmeat—meat obtained by hunting wild animals, often ones that are endangered or protected

camera trap—a remotely activated camera equipped with a motion sensor or an infrared sensor, used to capture images of wildlife with as little human interference as possible

captive breeding—the process of breeding wild animals in controlled environments such as wildlife reserves, zoos, botanical gardens and other conservation facilities, especially animals that have become rare in the wild

carbon dioxide—an invisible, colorless gas, formed by burning fuels, the breakdown or burning of animal and plant matter, and the act of breathing, that is absorbed from the air by plants in photosynthesis

climate change—changes in the world's weather, particularly a rise in temperature, thought to be caused by things such as increased levels of carbon dioxide in the atmosphere produced by the use of fossil fuels

citizen science—scientific work undertaken by members of the general public, often in collaboration with or under the direction of professional scientists and scientific institutions

conservationist—a person who works to protect or conserve wildlife and the environment

contaminant—any potentially undesirable substance (physical, chemical or biological) that makes something impure; usually refers to the introduction of harmful human-made substances

DDT—a poisonous substance used for killing insects

ecosystem—a complex network involving all living organisms interacting with the nonliving components of their environment

ecosystem services—the direct and indirect benefits to humans of healthily functioning ecosystems, including provisioning (such as supplying food and water), regulating (such as controlling climate and disease), supporting (forming soil, producing oxygen, etc.) and cultural (recreational and spiritual contributions)

endangered species—a plant or animal species existing in such small numbers that it is in danger of becoming extinct in the wild

environmental DNA (eDNA)—DNA released from an organism into the environment from such sources as feces, mucous, shed skin and hair, and carcasses

extinct—no longer existing in the wild

extirpated—no longer existing in a specified geographic area but occurring elsewhere

feral—having escaped domestication and become wild, such as feral cats

food web—the network of interconnected food chains in an ecosystem (a food chain describes the order in which organisms or living things depend on each other for food in an ecosystem)

fledgling—a young bird that is learning to fly

fossil fuels—sources of energy, such as coal, oil and natural gas, formed by plants and animal remains and buried in the earth over millions of years

fungi (plural of *fungus*)—the organisms of the kingdom Fungi, which includes yeasts, rusts, smuts, mildews, molds and mushrooms

grasslands—areas that are generally open and flat, dominated by various kinds of grasses and with few or no trees. There are two types of grasslands: temperate and tropical. One such tropical grassland is the African savanna.

greenhouse gases—gases in our atmosphere, including carbon dioxide and methane, that absorb infrared radiation, trap heat in the atmosphere and contribute to the greenhouse effect. Human activities such as the burning of fossil fuels are increasing the amount of greenhouse gases in the atmosphere.

habitat—the natural place where plants, animals and other organisms are most suited to live and breed

heavy metals—metals naturally found in the earth that can become concentrated as a result of human-caused activities and are noted for their potential toxic impacts on human health and the environment. They include cadmium, mercury, lead and arsenic.

hydrophone—a device used to detect or monitor sounds underwater, such as the sound made by whales

invasive species—plants and animals from other places that are not native to a particular area and cause harm to the local environment and to the plants and animals that *are* native to the area

keystone species—a species that has a major influence on the way an ecosystem works such that if it were removed, the ecosystem would change drastically

line transect—survey that involves an observer traveling along a designated line of given length to measure the distribution of organisms

mass extinction—when a large number of species become extinct within a relatively short period due to drastic environmental changes or a catastrophic global event

microplastics—extremely small pieces of plastic in the environment, resulting from the disposal and breakdown of consumer products and industrial waste, which can be harmful to the ocean and aquatic life

native species—species that occur naturally in a particular area or habitat

neonicotinoids—a special class of pesticides that has been linked to the rapid decline of many wild pollinator species

nocturnal—animals active only at night

ocean acidification—changes in the chemistry of the ocean when carbon dioxide being absorbed by the ocean reacts with the seawater to produce acid. It is caused primarily by excess carbon dioxide in the atmosphere.

old-growth forest—a forest dominated by old trees that has developed over a long period of time without significant disturbance and has unique ecological and structural features such as diversity in plant and animal species

pathogen—an organism such as a type of bacteria or virus that causes diseases

pesticide—a chemical used to kill pests such as insects that attack crops

poaching—the illegal catching or killing of an animal on someone else's land or in contravention of official protection

pollinator—organism that transfers pollen from one plant to another, allowing seeds to develop

pollution—the presence of harmful chemicals or other substances in the environment

predator—an animal that hunts other animals for food

prey—an animal that is hunted and eaten by other animals

range—species range is the native geographic area in which an organism can be found. Range also refers to the geographic distribution of a particular species.

reptile—a vertebrate, cold-blooded animal of a class that includes snakes, lizards, crocodiles, alligators, turtles and tortoises

salinity—a measure of the amount of salt dissolved in water

species—a group of closely related organisms that share similar characteristics and are capable of producing offspring

terrestrial—living on land rather than in water or air

wetland—a land area where the soil is permanently or seasonally saturated with water

zooplankton—tiny aquatic organisms that float near the surface of water and on which other sea creatures feed. Along with phytoplankton, zooplankton are key components of marine ecosystems forming the base of most marine food webs.

RESOURCES

PRINT

Alexander, Jane. *Wild Things, Wild Places: Adventurous Tales of Wildlife and Conservation on Planet Earth.* New York, NY: Alfred A. Knopf, 2016.

Carson, Rachel. *Silent Spring.* Boston, MA: Houghton Mifflin, 1962; Mariner Books, 2002.

Flach, Tim, and Sam Wells. *Endangered.* New York, NY: Abrams, 2017.

Fossey, Dian. *Gorillas in the Mist.* Boston, MA: Mariner Books, 2000 (paperback ed.).

Goodall, Jane, with Thane Maynard and Gail Hudson. *Hope for Animals and Their World: How Endangered Species Are Being Rescued from the Drink.* New York, NY: Grand Central Publishing, 2009.

Groc, Isabelle. *Gentle Giants: An Emotional Face to Face with Dolphins and Whales.* Palo Alto, CA: White Star Publishers, 2011.

Lawrence, Anthony, and Graham Spence. *The Elephant Whisperer: My Life with the Herd in the African Wild.* New York, NY: St. Martin's Griffin, 2012.

Moore, Robin. *In Search of Lost Frogs: The Quest to Find the World's Rarest Amphibians.* Richmond Hill, ON: Firefly Books, 2014.

McKenna, Virginia. *The Life in My Years.* London, UK: Oberon Books, 2010.

Safina, Carl. *Beyond Words: What Animals Think and Feel.* New York, NY: Picador, 2016 (reprint ed.).

Sartore, Joel. *The Photo Ark: One Man's Quest to Document the World's Animals.* Des Moines, IA: National Geographic, 2017.

Scardina, Julie, and Jeff Flocken. *Wildlife Heroes: 40 Leading Conservationists and the Animals They Are Committed to Saving.* Philadelphia, PA: Running Press, 2012.

Sheldrick, Daphne. *An African Love Story: Love, Life And Elephants.* London, UK: Penguin UK, 2013.

Winter, Steve, and Sharon Guynup. *Tigers Forever: Saving the World's Most Endangered Big Cat.* Des Moines, IA: National Geographic, 2013.

ONLINE

Amphibian Survival Alliance: amphibians.org
Audubon: audubon.org
Australian Koala Foundation: savethekoala.com
BirdLife International: birdlife.org
Born Free Foundation: bornfree.org.uk
Center for Biological Diversity: biologicaldiversity.org
Cornell Lab of Ornithology: birds.cornell.edu
David Suzuki Foundation: davidsuzuki.org
EDGE of Existence Programme: edgeofexistence.org
Galapagos Conservancy: galapagos.org

International Fund for Animal Welfare: ifaw.org
IUCN Red List of Threatened Species: iucnredlist.org
Jane Goodall's Roots & Shoots: rootsandshoots.org
Living Planet Index: livingplanetindex.org
San Diego Zoo Kids: kids.sandiegozoo.org
TRAFFIC (Wildlife Trade Monitoring Network): traffic.org
Whale and Dolphin Conservation: whales.org
Wilderness Committee: wildernesscommittee.org
Wildscreen ARKive: arkive.org
World Wildlife Fund: worldwildlife.org

ACKNOWLEDGMENTS

This book owes its existence to the knowledge, passion, commitment and kindness of many people, and I am very grateful to all the individuals who helped make this project happen.

First and foremost, I would like to thank Orca Book Publishers for considering a book on endangered species, and particularly my editor, Sarah Harvey, for her kindness, patience and encouragement and for guiding me through the process and making all of this happen. Many thanks to Jennifer Playford for her beautiful design.

I would like to thank all the people who work hard to conserve endangered species in every corner of the world. I would also like to express my gratitude for all the wild species of the world. Seeing them or just simply knowing they are there has given me a true sense of connection and purpose, and continually brings me joy and peace.

I would like to mention one special individual who has been in my thoughts while writing this book: Gwen Barlee, who was the Wilderness Committee's policy director. Gwen and I shared amazing adventures, looking for the most elusive species of British Columbia. She was a fearless advocate for endangered species, and I truly hope this book will inspire younger generations to carry the torch and fight for the future of wild spaces and species.

Over the last ten years I have had the immense privilege to work with many remarkable conservationists and scientists, people who kindly offered their time in the field and others who were generous with sharing their research and passion about the natural world.

In particular I would like to mention Jack Orr, former project lead with the Arctic Research Division of Fisheries and Oceans Canada, who welcomed me as part of his team on two field science expeditions in Nunavut and Manitoba, allowing me the exceptional opportunity to immerse myself in the world of belugas and narwhals. I would also like to thank the Oregon Spotted Frog Recovery Team, Monica Pearson, and the Fraser Valley Conservancy for sharing their knowledge of amphibians, particularly the precious frog, and the fragile wetland habitats they rely on to survive. I would like to thank the committed scientists and their teams who have tirelessly worked for decades to conserve the endangered North Atlantic right whale and spent time with me in the field: Moira Brown and Scott Kraus of the Anderson Cabot Center for Ocean Life at the New England Aquarium, Stormy Mayo and Scott Landry of the Center for Coastal Studies, Timothy Cole of the National Oceanic and Atmospheric Administration and Doug Nowacek of Duke University Marine Lab. I am grateful to Dr. Laurie Marker and her team, who welcomed me and my daughter at the Cheetah Conservation Fund in Namibia; Ellen Hines of San Francisco State University, who invited me to be part of her dedicated and fun group of international female scientists looking for rare dolphins in the Gulf of Thailand; Tim Tinker of the US Geological Survey, who welcomed me on a sea otter field-research project in California and shared his passion on everything otter related; Robin Baird with Cascadia Research, who introduced me to the world of marine mammals in Hawaii and shared his knowledge of southern resident killer whales in the Puget Sound waters. I am also truly appreciative of the assistance of the Monterey Bay Aquarium, the Environmental Youth Alliance and the Vancouver Aquarium.

I am grateful for having been able to spend time in the field in various parts of British Columbia with local biologists who shared their knowledge of different species at risk: Christine Bishop, Mike Mackintosh, Lauren Meads, the Burrowing Owl Conservation Society, West Moberly and Saulteau First Nations, Chris Johnson, Scott McNay, Brian Pate, Melissa Todd, Heath Smith, Conservation Canines, Andrea Gielens, Sofi Hindmarch, David Hancock and many, many more. Over the years I have been inspired by local conservationists dedicated to making a difference in their backyard: Dick and Steve Clegg, Alexandra Morton, Betty Krawczyk, to name only a few.

I am also truly appreciative of the assistance of the Monterey Bay Aquarium, the Vancouver Aquarium and the Environmental Youth Alliance.

Lastly and above all, my deepest thanks to my family, who was always there for me, supported this journey with patience, humor and love, and kindly allowed me to share my enthusiasm and curiosity for the wild with them.

INDEX

*Page numbers in **bold** indicate an image caption.*